H37
1986

KEPT FOR THE MASTER'S USE

FRANCES R. HAVERGAL

While this book is designed for
your personal enjoyment,
it is also intended for group study.
A Leader's Guide with Victor
Multiuse Transparency Masters
is available from your local bookstore
or from the publisher.

VICTOR BOOKS a division of SP Publications, Inc.

WHEATON, ILLINOIS 60187

Offices also in
Whitby, Ontario, Canada
Amersham-on-the-Hill, Bucks, England

The Classic Electives from Victor Books
Getting Things from God by Charles A. Blanchard
Inherit the Kingdom by F.B. Meyer
Kept for the Master's Use by Frances R. Havergal
With Christ in the School of Obedience by Andrew Murray

Scripture quotations in this book are from the
King James Version of the Bible.

Recommended Dewey Decimal Classification: 248.4
Suggested Subject Heading: CHRISTIAN LIFE

Library of Congress Catalog Card Number: 85-62707
ISBN: 0-89693-279-6

VICTOR BOOKS
A division of SP Publications, Inc.
Wheaton, Illinois 60187

CONTENTS

1. Our Lives Kept for Jesus 7
2. Our Moments Kept for Jesus 24
3. Our Hands Kept for Jesus 32
4. Our Feet Kept for Jesus...................................42
5. Our Voices Kept for Jesus 47
6. Our Lips Kept for Jesus 57
7. Our Silver and Gold Kept for Jesus.................68
8. Our Intellects Kept for Jesus...........................77
9. Our Wills Kept for Jesus 82
10. Our Hearts Kept for Jesus 88
11. Our Love Kept for Jesus...................................93
12. Our Selves Kept for Jesus.................................98
13. Christ for Us 105

KEPT FOR
THE MASTER'S USE

Take my life, and let it be
Consecrated, Lord, to Thee.

Take my moments and my days;
Let them flow in ceaseless praise.

Take my hands, and let them move
At the impulse of Thy love.

Take my feet, and let them be
Swift and "beautiful" for Thee.

Take my voice, and let me sing
Always, only, for my King.

Take my lips, and let them be
Filled with messages from Thee.

Take my silver and my gold;
Not a mite would I withhold.

Take my intellect, and use
Every power as Thou shalt choose.

Take my will and make it Thine:
It shall be no longer mine.

Take my heart; it *is* Thine own,
It shall be Thy royal throne.

Take my love; my Lord, I pour
At Thy feet its treasure-store.

Take myself, and I will be
Ever, *only*, ALL for Thee.

CHAPTER ONE

OUR LIVES
KEPT FOR JESUS

"Keep my life, that it may be
Consecrated, Lord, to Thee."

M

Many a heart has echoed the little song:

Take my life, and let it be
Consecrated, Lord, to Thee!

And yet those echoes have not been, in every case and at all times, so clear and full and firm, so continuously glad as we would wish, and perhaps expected. Some of us have said,

I launch me forth upon a sea
Of boundless love and tenderness;

and after a little while we have found or fancied that there is a hidden leak in our vessel, and though we are doubtless still afloat, yet we are not sailing with the same free, exultant confidence as at first. What is it that has dulled and weakened the echo of our consecration song? What is the little leak that hinders the swift and buoyant course of our consecrated life? Holy Father, let Thy loving Spirit guide the hand that writes, and strengthen the heart of every one who reads what shall be written, for Jesus' sake.

While many a sorrowfully varied answer to these questions may, and probably will, arise from touched and sensitive consciences, each being shown by God's faithful Spirit the special sin, the special yielding to temptation which has hindered and spoiled the blessed life which he or she sought to enter and enjoy, it seems to me that one or other of two things has lain at the outset of the failure and disappointment.

First, it may have arisen from want of the simplest belief in the simplest fact, as well as want of trust in one of the simplest and plainest words our gracious Master ever uttered! The unbelieved fact being simply that He hears us; the untrusted word being one of those plain, broad foundation-stones on which we rested our whole weight, it may be many years ago, and which we had no idea we ever doubted, or were in any danger of doubting now— "Him that cometh to Me I will in no wise cast out" (John 6:37).

"Take my life!" We may have said it or sung it before the Lord many times; but if it were only once whispered in His ear with full purpose of heart, should we not believe that He heard it? And if we know that He heard it, should we not believe that He has answered it, and ful-

8

filled this, our heart's desire? For with Him hearing means heeding. Then why should we doubt that He did certainly take our lives when we offered them, our bodies when we presented them? Have we not been wronging His faithfulness all this time by practically, even if unconsciously, doubting whether the prayer ever really reached Him? And if so, is it any wonder that we have not realized all the power and joy of full consecration? By some means or other He has to teach us to trust implicitly at every step of the way. And so, if we did not really trust in this matter, He has had to let us find out our want of trust by withholding the sensible part of the blessing, and thus stirring us up to find out why it is withheld.

An offered gift must be either accepted or refused. Can He have refused it when He has said, "Him that cometh to Me I will in no wise cast out"? If not, then it must have been accepted. It is just the same process as when we came to Him first of all, with the intolerable burden of our sins. There was no help for it but to come with them to Him, and take His Word for it that He would not and did not cast us out. And so coming, so believing, we found rest for our souls; we found that His Word was true, and that His taking away our sins was a reality.

Some give their lives to Him then and there, and go forth to live not at all unto themselves, but unto Him who died for them. This is as it should be, for conversion and consecration ought to be simultaneous. But practically it is not very often so, except with those in whom the bringing out of darkness into marvelous light has been sudden and dazzling, and full of deepest contrasts. More frequently the work resembles the case of the Hebrew servant de-

9

scribed in Exodus 21:1-6, who, after six years' experience of a good master's service, dedicates himself voluntarily, unreservedly, and irrevocably to it, saying, "I love my master; I will not go free"; the master then accepting and sealing him to lifelong service, free in law yet bound in love. This seems to be a figure of later consecration founded on experience and love.

And yet, as at our first coming, it is less than nothing, worse than nothing that we have to bring; for our lives, even our redeemed and pardoned lives, are not only weak and worthless, but defiled and sinful. But thanks be to God for the living altar that sanctifies the gift, even our Lord Jesus Christ Himself! By Him we draw nigh unto God; to Him, as one with the Father, we offer our living sacrifice; in Him, as the beloved of the Father, we know it is accepted. So, dear friends, when once He has created in us the desire to be altogether His own, and put into our hearts the prayer, "Take my life," let us go on our way rejoicing, believing that He *has* taken our lives, our hands, our feet, our voices, our intellects, our wills, our whole selves, to be ever, only, all for Him. Let us consider that a blessedly settled thing; not because of anything we have felt, or said, or done, but because we know that He hears us, and because we know that He is true to His Word.

If our hearts do not condemn us in this matter, our disappointment may arise from another cause. It may be that we have not received because we have not asked a fuller and further blessing. Suppose that we did believe, thankfully and surely, that the Lord heard our prayer, and that He did indeed answer and accept us, and set us apart for Himself, and yet we find that our consecration

OUR LIVES KEPT FOR JESUS

was not merely miserably incomplete, but that we have drifted back again almost to where we were before. Or suppose things are not quite as bad as that, still we have not quite all we expected; and even if we think we can truly say, "O God, my heart is fixed," we find, to our daily sorrow, that somehow or other the details of our conduct do not seem to be fixed; something or other is perpetually slipping through, till we get perplexed and distressed. Then we are tempted to wonder whether, after all, there was not some mistake about it, and the Lord did not really take us at our word, although we took Him at His Word. And then the struggle with one doubt and entanglement and temptation only seems to land us in another. What is to be done then?

Clean Before the Lord

First, very humbly and utterly honestly we need to search and try our ways before our God; or rather, as we shall soon realize our helplessness to make such a search, ask Him to do it for us, praying for His promised Spirit to show us unmistakably if there is any secret thing within us that is hindering both the inflow and outflow of His grace to us and through us. Do not let us shrink into a dark corner from some unexpected flash; do not let us wince at the sudden touching of a hidden plague spot. The Lord always does His own work thoroughly, if we will only let Him do it. If we put ourselves into His hands, He will search and probe fully and firmly, though very tenderly. It may be painful, but only that He may do the very thing we want—cleanse us and heal us thoroughly, so that we may set off to walk in real newness of life. But if we do not put it unreservedly into His hands, it will be no use thinking or talking about our lives being consecrated to Him. The heart that is not entrusted to Him for searching will not be undertaken by Him for cleansing; the life that fears to come to the light lest any deed should be reproved can never know the blessedness and the privileges of walking in the light.

But what then? When He has graciously again put a new song into our mouth, and we are singing,

> Ransomed, healed, restored, forgiven,
> Who like me His praise should sing?

and again with fresh earnestness we are saying,

> Take my life, and let it be
> Consecrated, Lord, to Thee!

are we only to look forward to the same disappointing experience over again? Are we always to stand at the threshold? Consecration is not so much a step as a course; not so much an act as a position to which a course of action inseparably belongs. Insofar as it is a course and a position, there must naturally be a definite entrance upon it, and a time, it may be a moment, when that entrance is made. That is when we say, "Take"; but we do not want to go on taking a first step over and over again. What we want now is to be maintained in that position, and to fulfill that course. So let us go on to another prayer. Having already said, "Take my life, for I cannot give it to Thee," let us now say, with deepened conviction that without Christ we really can do nothing—"*Keep* my life, for I cannot keep it for Thee."

Let us ask this with the same simple trust to which, in so many other things, He has so liberally and graciously responded. For "this is the confidence that we have in Him, that if we ask anything according to His will, He hears us; and if we know that He heareth us, whatsoever we ask, we know that we have the petitions that we desired of Him" (1 John 5:14-15). There can be no doubt that this petition is according to His will, because it is based on many a promise. May I give it to you just as it floats through my own mind again and again, knowing whom I have believed, and being persuaded that He is *able to keep* that which I have committed unto Him?

Keep my life, that it may be
Consecrated, Lord, to Thee.

Keep my moments and my days;
Let them flow in ceaseless praise.

Keep my hands, that they may move
At the impulse of Thy love.

Keep my feet, that they may be
Swift and "beautiful" for Thee.

Keep my voice, that I may sing
Always, only, for my King.

Keep my lips, that they may be
Filled with messages from Thee.

Keep my silver and my gold;

13

Not a mite would I withhold.

Keep my intellect, and use
Every power as Thou shalt choose.

Keep my will, O keep it Thine;
For it is no longer mine.

Keep my heart; it *is* Thine own,
It is now Thy royal throne.

Keep my love; my Lord, I pour
At Thy feet its treasure-store.

Keep myself, that I may be
Ever, *only*, ALL for Thee.

Yes! He who is able and willing to *take unto* Himself is no less able and willing to *keep for* Himself. Our willing offering has been made by His enabling grace, and this our King has seen with joy. And now we pray, "Keep this forever in the imagination of the thoughts of the heart of Thy people" (1 Chron. 29:17-18).

This blessed *taking* once for all, which we may quietly believe to be an accomplished fact, followed by the continual *keeping*, for which He will be continually inquired of by us, seems analogous to the great washing away of sins which Christ offers through salvation and the repeated cleansing of sins for which we need to be continually coming to Him. For with the deepest and sweetest consciousness that He has indeed taken our lives to be His very own, the need of His active and actual keeping of them in every detail and at every moment is most fully realized. But then we have the promise of our faithful God, "I, the Lord, do keep it . . . I will keep it night and day" (Isa. 27:3). The only question is, will we trust this promise, or will we not? If we do, we shall find it come true. If not, of course it will not be realized. For unclaimed promises are like uncashed checks; they will keep us from bankruptcy, but not from want. But if not, *why* not? What right have we to pick out one of His faithful sayings, and say we don't expect Him to fulfill that? What defense can we bring, what excuse can we invent, for so doing?

If you appeal to experience against His faithfulness to His Word, I will appeal to experience too, and ask: Did you ever *really trust* Jesus to fulfill any word of His to you and find your trust deceived? As to the past experience of the details of your life not being kept for Jesus, look a little more closely at it, and you will find that though you may have asked, you did not trust. Whatever you did really trust Him to keep, He has kept, and the unkept things were never really entrusted. Scrutinize this past experience as you will, and it will only bear witness against your unfaithfulness, never against His absolute faithfulness.

Yet this witness must not be unheeded. We must not forget the things that are behind till they are confessed and forgiven. Let us now bring all this unsatisfactory past experience and, most of all, the want of trust which has been the poison spring of its course to the precious blood of Christ, which cleanses us from all sin, even this sin. Perhaps we never saw that we were not trusting Jesus as He deserves to be trusted; if so, let us wonderingly hate ourselves the more that we could be so trustless to such a Saviour, and so sinfully dark and stupid that we did not

15

even see it. And oh, let us wonderingly love Him the more that He has been so patient and gentle with us, upbraiding not, though in our slow-hearted foolishness we have been grieving Him by this subtle unbelief; and then by His grace, may we enter upon a new era of experience, our lives kept for Him more fully than ever before, because we trust Him more simply and unreservedly to keep them!

The Error of Self-dependence

Here we must face a question, and perhaps a difficulty. Does it not almost seem as if we were at this point led to trusting our trust, making everything hinge upon it, and thereby only removing a subtle dependence on ourselves one step further back, disguising instead of renouncing it? If Christ's *keeping* depends on our *trusting*, and our continuing to trust depends on ourselves, we are in no better or safer position than before, and shall only be landed in a fresh series of disappointments. The old story, something for the sinner to *do*, crops up again here, only with the ground shifted from works to trust. As a friend said to me, "I see now! I did trust Jesus to do everything else for me, but I thought that this trusting was something that *I* had to do." And so, of course, what she had to do had been a perpetual effort and frequent failure. We can no more trust and keep on trusting than we can do anything else of ourselves. Even in this it must be "Jesus only." We are not to look to Him only to be the author and finisher of our faith, but we are to look to Him for all the intermediate fulfillment of the work of faith (2 Thes. 1:11), committing even this to His power.

For we both may and must
Commit our very faith to Him,
Entrust to Him our trust.

What a long time it takes us to come down to the
conviction, and still more to the realization, of the fact
that without Him we can do *nothing*, but that He must
work *all* our works in us! "This is the work of God, that ye
believe on Him whom He has sent" (John 6:29). And no
less must it be the work of God that we go on believing,
and that we go on trusting. Then, dear friends, who are
longing to trust Him with unbroken and unwavering
trust, cease the effort and drop the burden, and *now*
entrust your trust to Him! He is just as well able to keep
that as any other part of the complex lives which we want
Him to take and keep for Himself. And oh, do not pass on
content with the thought, "Yes, that is a good idea; perhaps I would find that a great help!" *But do it now.* It is no
help to the sailor to see a flash of light across a dark sea, if
he does not instantly steer accordingly.

Consecration is not a religiously selfish thing. If it sinks
into that, it ceases to be consecration. We want our lives
kept, not that we may feel happy, and be saved the
distress consequent on wandering, and get the power
with God and man, and all the other privileges linked
with it. We shall have all this, because the lower is includ-
ed in the higher; but our true aim, if the love of Christ
constrains us, will be far beyond this. Not for "me" at all,
but "for Jesus"; not for my safety, but for His glory; not
for my comfort, but for His joy; not that I may find rest,
but that He may see the travail of His soul and be satis-

fied! Yes, for *Him* I want to be kept. Kept for His use; kept to be His witness; kept for His joy! Kept for Him, that in me He may show forth some tiny sparkle of His light and beauty; kept to do His will and His work in His own way; kept (it may be) to suffer for His sake; kept for Him, that He may do just what He wants with me; kept, so that no other lord shall have any more dominion over me, but that Jesus shall have all there is to have—little enough, indeed, but not divided or diminished by any other claim. Is not this, O you who love the Lord—is not this worth living for, worth asking for, worth trusting for?

This is consecration, and I cannot begin to tell you the blessedness of it. It is not the least use arguing with one who has had but a taste of its blessedness, and saying to him, "How can these things be?" It is not the least use starting all sorts of difficulties and theoretical supposi- tions about it with such a one, any more than it was when the Jews argued with the man who said, "One thing I know, that whereas I was blind now I see" (John 9:25). The Lord Jesus does take the life that is offered to Him, and He does keep the life for Himself that is entrusted to Him; but until the life is offered we cannot know the taking, and until the life is entrusted we cannot know or understand the keeping. All we can do is to say, "Oh, taste and see!" and bear witness to the reality of Jesus Christ, that we have found Him true to His every word, and that we have proved Him able even to do exceeding abundantly above all we asked or thought. Why should we hesitate to bear this testimony? We have done nothing at all; we have, in all our efforts, only proved to ourselves, and perhaps to others, that we had no power either to give or keep our lives. Why should we not, then, glorify His grace by acknowledging that we have found Him so wonderfully and tenderly gracious and faithful in both taking and keeping as we never supposed or imagined? I shall never forget the smile and emphasis with which a poor workingman bore this witness to his Lord. I said to him:

"Well, H., we have a good Master, have we not?"

"Ah," he said, "a good deal better than ever *I* thought!"

That summed up his experience, and so it will sum up the experience of all who will but yield their lives wholly to the same good Master.

The Choice of Consecration

I cannot close this chapter without a word to those, especially my younger friends, who, though they have named the name of Christ, are saying: "Yes, this is all very well for some people, or for older people, but I am not ready for it; I can't say I see my way to this sort of thing."

I am going to take the lowest ground for a minute and appeal to *your* past experience. Are you satisfied with your experience of the other "sort of thing"? Your pleasant pursuits, your harmless recreations, your nice occupations, even your improving ones; what fruit are you having from them? Your social intercourse, your daily talks and walks, your investments of all the time that remains to you over and above the absolute duties God may have given you; what fruit that shall remain have you from all this? Day after day passes on, and year after year, and what shall the harvest be? What is even the present return? Are you getting any real and lasting satisfaction out

19

of it all? Are you not finding that things lose their flavor and that you are spending your strength day after day for nothing? That you are no more satisfied than you were a year ago—rather less so, if anything? Does not a sense of hollowness and weariness come over you as you go on in the same round, perpetually getting through things only to begin again? It cannot be otherwise. Over even the freshest and purest earthly fountains the Hand that never makes a mistake has written, "Whosoever drinketh of this water shall thirst again" (John 4:13). Look into your own heart and you will find a copy of that inscription already traced, "Shall thirst again." And the characters are being deepened with every attempt to quench the inevitable thirst and weariness in life, which can only be satisfied and rested in full consecration to God; for as Augustine has said, "Thou hast made us *for Thyself*, and the heart never resteth till it findeth rest in Thee." I tell you of a brighter and happier life, whose inscription is, "Shall never thirst," a life that is no dull round-and-round in a circle of unsatisfactoriness, but a life that has found its true and entirely satisfactory center, and set itself toward a shining and entirely satisfactory goal, whose brightness is cast over every step of the way. Will you not seek it?

Do not shrink, and suspect, and hang back from what it may involve, with selfish and unconfiding and ungenerous halfheartedness. Take the word of any who have willingly offered themselves unto the Lord, that the life of consecration is a good deal better than they thought! Choose this day whom you will serve with real, thoroughgoing, wholehearted service, and He will receive you; and you will find, as we have found, that He is such a good

Master that you are satisfied with His goodness, and that you will never want to go out free. Nay, rather take His own word for it; He says: "If they obey and serve Him, they shall spend their days in prosperity, and their years in pleasures" (Job 36:11). You cannot possibly understand that till you are really *in* His service! For He does not give, nor even show, His wages before you enter it. And He says, "My servants shall sing for joy of heart" (Isa. 65:14). But you cannot begin to sing that song to see what it is like, you cannot even read one bar of it, till your nominal or even promised service is exchanged for real and undivided consecration. But when He can call you His servant, then you will find yourself singing for joy of heart, because He says you shall.

Do not think that because you do not understand all consecration may include, you are therefore not qualified for it. I daresay it comprehends a great deal more than either you or I understand, but we can both enter into the spirit of it, and the detail will unfold itself as long as our probation shall last. Christ demands a hearty consecration in *will*, and He will teach us what that involves in *act*.

This explains the paradox that full consecration may be in one sense the act of a moment, and in another the work of a lifetime. It must be complete to be real, and yet, if real, it is always incomplete; a point of rest, and yet a perpetual progression.

Suppose you sell a piece of ground to another person. You give it up, then and there, entirely to that other; it is no longer in your own possession; you no longer dig and sow, plant and reap at your discretion or for your own profit. His occupation of it is total; no other has any right to an inch of it; it is his affair thereafter what crops to arrange for and how to make the most of it. But his practical occupation of it may not appear all at once. There may be wasteland which he will take into full cultivation only by degrees, space wasted for want of draining or by overfencing, and odd corners lost for want of enclosing; fields yielding smaller returns than they might because of hedgerows too wide and shady, trees too many and spreading, and strips of good soil trampled into uselessness for want of undefined pathways.

Just so it is with our lives. The transaction (so to speak) of becoming God's child is definite and complete. But then begins the practical development of consecration. And here He leads on softly, as His children are able to endure. I do not suppose anyone sees all that it involves at the outset. We have not a notion what an amount of wasted power there has been in our lives; we never measured out the odd corners and the undrained bits, and it never occurred to us what good fruit might be grown in our straggling hedgerows, nor how the shade of our trees has been keeping the sun from the scanty crops. And so, season by season, we shall be sometimes more than a little startled, yet always very glad, as we find that bit by bit the Master shows how much more may be made of our ground, how much more He is able to make of it than we did; and we shall be willing to work under Him and do exactly what He points out, even if it comes to cutting down a shady tree or clearing out a ditch full of pretty weeds and wildflowers.

As the seasons pass, it will seem as if there is always more and more to be done, for the fact is that He is constantly showing us something more to be done in it, proving that it is really His ground. Only let Him *have* the ground, no matter how poor or overgrown the soil may be, and then He will make her wilderness like Eden, and her desert like the garden of the Lord. Yes, even *our* desert! And then we shall sing, "My beloved is gone down into *his* garden, to the beds of spices, to feed in the gardens and to gather lilies" (Song 6:2, italics added).

Made for Thyself, O God!
Made for Thy love, Thy service, Thy delight;
Made to show forth Thy wisdom, grace, and might;
Made for Thy praise, whom veiled archangels laud;
O, strange and glorious thought, that we may be
A joy to Thee?

Yet the heart turns away
From this grand destiny of bliss, and deems
'Twas made for its poor self, for passing dreams,
Chasing illusions melting day by day,
Till for ourselves we read on this world's best,
"This is not rest!"

CHAPTER TWO

OUR MOMENTS
KEPT FOR JESUS

"Keep my moments and my days;
Let them flow in ceaseless praise."

I t may be helpful
to writer and reader if we consider some of the practical
details of the life which we desire to have "kept for Jesus"
in the order of the little hymn at the beginning of this
book, with the one word "take" changed to "keep." So
we will take a couplet for each chapter.

A Treasure Called Time

The first point that naturally comes up is that which is
almost synonymous with life—*our time.* And this brings
us at once face to face with one of our past difficulties, and
its probable cause.

When we take a wide sweep, we are so apt to be vague.
When we are aiming at generalities, we do not hit the
practicalities. We forget that faithfulness to principle is
only proved by faithfulness in detail. Has not this vague

ness had something to do with the constant ineffective-
ness of our feeble desire that our time should be devoted
to God?

In spiritual things, the greater does not always include
the less, but, paradoxically, the less more often includes
the greater. So in this case, time is entrusted to us to be
used for our Lord. But we cannot grasp it as a whole. We
instinctively break it up in order to deal with it for any
purpose. So when a new year comes around, we commit
it with special earnestness to the Lord. But as we do so,
are we not conscious of a feeling that even a year is too
much for us to deal with? And does not this feeling, that
we are dealing with a larger thing than we can grasp, take
away from the sense of reality? Thus we are brought to a
more manageable measure; and as the Sunday mornings
or the Monday mornings come around, we thankfully
commit the beginning of the week to Him, and the sense
of help and rest is renewed and strengthened. But not
even the six or seven days are close enough to our hand;
even tomorrow exceeds our tiny grasp, and even tomorrow's grace is therefore not given to us. So we find the
need of considering our lives on a day-by-day basis; any
more general committal and consecration of our time will
not do. Here we have found much comfort and help, and
if results have not been entirely satisfactory, they have, at
least, been more so than before we reached this point of
subdivision.

But if we have found help and blessing by going a
certain distance in one direction, is it not probable we
shall find more if we go farther in the same? And so, if we
may commit the days to our Lord, why not the hours, and

why not the moments? And may we not expect a fresh and special blessing in so doing?

We seldom realize the importance of moments. Only let us consider those two sayings of God about them, "In a moment shall they die" (Job 34:20) and, "We shall all be changed in a moment" (1 Cor. 15:52) and we shall think less lightly of them. Nothing seems less within the possibility of our own keeping, yet nothing is more inclusive of all other keeping. Therefore let us ask Him to keep them for us.

Are moments not the tiny joints through which the darts of temptation pierce us? Only give us time, we think, and we should not be overcome. Only give us time, and we could pray and resist, and the devil would flee from us. But he comes in a moment; and in a moment—an unguarded, unkept one—we utter the hasty or exaggerated word, or think the un-Christlike thought, or feel the un-Christlike impatience or resentment.

But even if we have gone so far as to say, "Take my moments," have we gone the step farther, and really *let* Him take them—really entrusted them to Him? It is no good saying "take" when we do not let go. How can another keep that which we are keeping hold of? So let us, with full trust in His power, first commit these slippery moments to Him—put them right into His hand—and then we may trustfully and happily say: "Lord, keep them for me! Keep every one of the quick series as it arises. I cannot keep them for Thee; do Thou keep them for Thyself!"

But the sanctified and Christ-loving heart cannot be satisfied with only negative keeping. We do not want only

26

to be kept from displeasing Him, but to be kept always pleasing Him. Every "kept *from*" should have its corresponding and still more blessed "kept *for*." We do not want our moments to be simply kept from Satan's use, but kept for the Lord's use; we want them to be not only kept from sin, but kept for His praise.

The Miracle of a Moment
Do you ask, "But what use can He make of mere moments?"

There is no need to prove or illustrate the obvious truth that, as are the moments, so will be the hours and the days which they build. You understand that well enough. I will answer your question as it stands.

Look back through the history of the church in all ages, and mark how often a great work and mighty influence grew out of a mere moment in the life of one of God's servants; a mere moment, but overshadowed and filled with the fruitful power of the Spirit of God. The moment may have been spent in uttering five words, but they have fed 5,000, or even 500,000. Or it may have been lit by the flash of a thought that has shone into hearts and homes throughout the land, and kindled torches that have been borne into earth's darkest corners. The rapid speaker or the lonely thinker little guessed what use his Lord was making of that single moment. There was no room in it for even a thought of that. If that moment had not been, though perhaps unconsciously, "kept for Jesus," but had been otherwise occupied, what a harvest to His praise would have been missed!

The same thing is going on every day. It is generally a

27

moment—either an opening or a culminating one—that really does the work. It is not so often a whole sermon as a single short sentence in it that wings God's arrow to a heart. It is seldom a whole conversation that is the means of bringing about the desired result, but some sudden turn of thought or word which comes with the electric touch of God's power. Sometimes it is less than that; only a look (and what is more momentary?) has been used by Him for the pulling down of strongholds. Again, in our own quiet waiting on God, as moment after moment glides past in the silence at His feet, the eye resting on a page of His Word, or only looking up to Him through the darkness, have we not found that He can so irradiate one passing moment with His light that its rays never die away, but shine on and on through days and years? Are not such moments proved to have been kept for Him? And if some, why not all?

Fractions of Eternity

This view of moments seems to make it clearer that it is impossible to serve two masters, for it is evident that the service of a moment cannot be divided. If it is occupied in the service of self, or any other master, it is not at the Lord's disposal; He cannot make use of what is already occupied.

Oh, how much we have missed by not placing them at His disposal! What might He not have done with the moments burdened with self or loaded with emptiness, which we have carelessly let drift by! Oh, what might have been if they had all been kept for Jesus! How He might have filled them with His light and life, enriching our own lives that have been impoverished by the waste, and using them in far-spreading blessing and power!

While we have been undervaluing these fractions of eternity, what has our gracious God been doing in them? How strangely touching are the words, "What is man that Thou shouldest set Thine heart upon him, and that Thou shouldest visit him every morning and *try him every moment?*" (Job 7:17-18, italics added) Terribly solemn and awful would be the thought that He has been trying us every moment, were it not for the yearning gentleness and love of the Father revealed in that wonderful expression of wonder, "What is man, that Thou shouldest set Thine heart upon him?" Think of that ceaseless setting of His heart upon us, careless and forgetful children as we have been! And then think of those other words, nonetheless literally true because given under a figure of speech: "I, the Lord, do keep it; *I will water it every moment*" (Isa. 27:3, italics added).

We see something of God's infinite greatness and wisdom when we try to fix our dazzled gaze on infinite space. But when we turn to the marvels of the microscope, we gain a clearer view and more definite grasp of these attributes by gazing on the perfection of His infinitesimal handiworks. Just so, while we cannot realize the infinite love which fills eternity, and the infinite vistas of the great future are dark even to the strongest telescopes of faith, we see that love magnified in the microscope of the moments, brought very close to us, and revealing its unspeakable perfection of detail to our wondering sight.

But we do not see this as long as the moments are kept in our own hands. We are like little children closing our

29

fingers over diamonds. How can the diamonds receive and reflect the rays of light while they are kept shut up tight in the dirty little hands? Give them up! Let our Father hold them for us and throw His own great light upon them. Then we shall see them full of fair colors of His manifold loving-kindnesses. Let Him always keep them for us, and then we shall always see His light and His love reflected in them.

And then surely they shall be filled with praise. Not that we are to be always singing hymns and using the expressions of other people's praise; but praise will be the tone, the color, the atmosphere in which they flow; none of them away from it or out of it.

Is it a little too much for them all to flow in ceaseless praise? Well, where will you stop? What proportion of your moments do you think enough for Jesus? How many for the spirit of praise, and how many for the spirit of heaviness? Be explicit about it, and come to an understanding. If He is not to have them all, then *how many?* Calculate balance, and apportion accordingly. You will not be able to do this in heaven—you know it will be all praise there; but you are free to halve your service of praise here or to make the proportion what you will.

Yet—He made you for His glory.

Yet—He chose you that you should be to the praise of His glory.

Yet—He loves you every moment, waters you every moment, watches you unslumberingly, cares for you unceasingly.

Yet—He died for you!

Dear friends, one can hardly write it without tears.

Shall you or I remember all this love and hesitate to give *all* our moments up to Him? Let us entrust them to Him, and ask Him to keep them all, every single one, for His own beloved self, and fill them *all* with His praise, and let them *all* be to His praise!

CHAPTER THREE

OUR HANDS
KEPT FOR JESUS

*"Keep my hands, that they may move
At the impulse of Thy love."*

When the Lord has said to us, "Is thine heart right, as My heart is with thy heart?" His next words seem to be, "If it be, give Me thine hand" (2 Kings 10:15).

What a call to confidence, and love, and free, loyal, happy service is this! And how different will the result of its acceptance be from the old lamentation: "We labor and have no rest; we have given the hand to the Egyptians and to the Assyrians" (Lam. 5:5-6). In the service of these other lords, under whatever shape they have presented themselves, we shall have known something of the meaning of having both the hands full with toil and affliction. How many a thing have we taken in hand (as we say) which we expected to find an agreeable task, an interest in life, a something toward filling up that unconfessed aching void, which is often most real when least acknowledged; and after a while we have found it change under our hands into irksome labor, involving perpetual trouble. The thing may have been of the earth and for the world, and then no wonder it failed to satisfy even the instinct of work, which comes naturally to many of us. Or it may have been right enough in itself, something for the good of others so far as we understood their good, and unselfish in all but unraveled motive; and yet we found it a tangled web because the hands that held it were not simply consecrated to God. Well, if so, let us bring these soiled and tangle-making hands to the Lord. Let us lift up our hearts with our hands to Him, asking Him to clear and cleanse them.

If He says, "What is that in thine hand?" let us examine honestly whether it is something which He can use for His glory or not. If not, do not let us hesitate an instant about dropping it. It may be something we do not like to part with; but the Lord is able to give us much more than this, and the first glimpse of the excellency of the knowledge of Christ Jesus our Lord will enable us to count those things loss which were gain to us.

But if it is something which He can use, He will make us do ever so much more with it than before. Moses little thought what the Lord was going to make him do with that rod in his hand! The first thing he had to do with it was to cast it on the ground, and see it pass through a startling change (it became a snake!). After this he was commanded to take it up again, hard and terrifying as it was to do so. But when it became again a rod in his hand, it was no longer what it was before, the simple rod of a wandering desert shepherd. Henceforth it was the rod of

God in his hand (Ex. 4:20), with which he would perform signs, and by which God Himself would do marvelous things (Ps. 78:12).

If we look at any Old Testament text about consecration, we shall see that the marginal reading of the word is "fill the hand" (e.g., Ex. 28:41; 1 Chron. 29:5). Now, if our hands are full of other things, they cannot be filled with the things that are Jesus Christ's; there must be emptying before there can be any true filling. So if we are sorrowfully seeing that our hands have not been kept for Jesus, let us humbly begin at the beginning, and ask Him to empty them thoroughly, that He may fill them completely.

For they *must* be emptied. Either we come to our Lord willingly about it, letting Him unclasp their hold, and gladly dropping the glittering weights they have been carrying, or, in very love, He will have to force them open, and wrench from the reluctant grasp the earthly things which are so occupying them that He cannot have His rightful use of them. There is only one other alternative, a terrible one—to be let alone till the day comes when not a gentle master, but the relentless king of terrors, shall empty the trembling hands as our feet follow him out of the busy world into the dark valley, for "it is certain we can carry nothing out" (1 Tim. 6:7).

Our Hands Belong to Jesus

All that has been said about consecration applies to our literal members. Look at your hand, the hand that holds this book as you read it. See how wonderfully it is made; how perfectly fitted for what it has to do; how ingeniously connected with the brain, so as to yield that instantaneous and instinctive obedience without which its beautiful mechanism would be very little good to us! *Your* hand, do you say? Whether it is soft and fair with an easy life, or rough and strong with a working one, or pale and weak with illness, it is the Lord Jesus Christ's. It is not your own at all; it belongs to Him. He made it, for without Him was not anything made that was made, not even your hand. And He has added the right of purchase—He has bought it that it might be one of His own instruments. We know this very well, but have we realized it? Have we really let Him use these hands of ours? Have we ever simply and sincerely asked Him to keep them for His own use?

Does this mean that we are always to be doing some definitely "religious" work, as it is called? No, but that *all that we do* is to be always definitely *done for Him*. There is a great difference. If the hands are indeed moving at the impulse of His love, the simplest little duties and acts are transfigured into holy service to the Lord.

A Christian schoolgirl loves Jesus; she wants to please Him all day long, and so she practices her piano scales carefully and conscientiously. It is at the impulse of His love that her fingers move so steadily through the otherwise tiresome exercises. Someday her Master will find a use for her music; but meanwhile it may be just as fruitfully done unto Him as if it were Ira Sankey at his organ, swaying the hearts of thousands.

The hand of a Christian lad traces the alphabet. He is doing his best because the teacher has stressed the importance of excellence. And so, for Jesus' sake, his hand moves accurately and perseveringly.

A busy wife, or daughter, or servant has a number of little manual duties to perform. If these are done slowly and leisurely, they may be got through, but there will not be time left for some little service to the poor, or some little kindness to a suffering or troubled neighbor, or for a quiet little time alone with God and His Word. And so the hands move quickly, impelled by the loving desire for service or communion, kept in busy motion for Jesus' sake. Or it may be that the special aim is to give no occasion of reproach to some who are watching, but so to adorn the doctrine that those may be won by the life who will not be won by the word. Then the hands will have their share to do. They will move carefully, neatly, perhaps even elegantly, making everything around as nice as possible, letting their intelligent touch be seen in the details of the home, and even of the dress, doing or arranging all the little things decently and in order for Jesus' sake. And so on with every duty in every position.

It may seem an odd idea, but a simple glance at one's hand, with the recollection, "This hand is not mine; it has been given to Jesus and it must be kept for Jesus," may sometimes tip the scale in a doubtful matter, and be a safeguard from certain temptations. With that thought fresh in your mind, as you look at your hand, can you let it take up things which, to say the very least, are not "for Jesus"? Things which evidently cannot be used, as they most certainly are not used, either for Him or by Him? Can you deliberately hold in your hand books of a kind which you know perfectly well, by sadly repeated experience, lead you farther from instead of nearer to Him? Books which must and do fill your mind with those other things which, entering in, choke the Word? Books which you would not care to read at all, if your heart were burning within you at the coming of His feet to bless you? Next time any temptation of this sort approaches, just *look at your hand!*

It was of a literal hand that our Lord Jesus spoke when He said, "Behold, the hand of him that betrayeth Me is with Me on the table" (Luke 22:21); and, "He that dippeth his hand with Me in the dish, the same shall betray Me" (Matt. 26:23). A hand so near to Jesus, with Him on the table, touching His own hand in the dish at that hour of sweetest and closest and most solemn intercourse, and yet betraying Him! That same hand taking the thirty pieces of silver! What a tremendous lesson of the need of keeping for our hands! Oh, that every hand that is with Him at His Communion table, and that takes the memorial bread, may be kept from any faithless and loveless motion!

And again, it was by literal wicked hands that our Lord Jesus was crucified and slain. Does not the thought that human hands have been so treacherous and cruel to our beloved Lord make us wish the more fervently that our hands may be totally and faithfully devoted to Him?

Temptations of the Hands

Danger and temptation to let the hands move at other impulses is every bit as great to those who have nothing else to do but to render direct service, and who think they are doing nothing else. Take one practical instance—our letter writing. Have we not been tempted (and fallen before the temptation), according to our various dispositions, to let the hand that holds the pen move at the impulse to write an unkind thought of another; or to say a clever and sarcastic thing, or a slightly colored and exaggerated thing, which will make our point more telling; or to let out a grumble or a suspicion; or to let the pen run away with us into flippant and trifling words, unworthy of our high and holy calling? Have we not drifted away from the golden reminder, "Should he reason with unprofitable talk, or with speeches wherewith he can do no good?" (Job 15:3) Why has this been, perhaps again and again? Is it not for want of putting our hands into our dear Master's hand, and asking and trusting Him to keep them? He *could* have kept; He *would* have kept!

Whatever our work or our special temptations may be, the principle remains the same, only let us apply it for ourselves.

Perhaps one hardly needs to say that the kept hands will be very gentle hands. Quick, angry motions of the heart will sometimes force themselves into expression by the hand, though the tongue may be restrained. The very way in which we close a door or lay down a book may be a victory or a defeat, a witness to Christ's keeping or a witness that we are not truly being kept. How can we expect that God will use this member as an instrument of righteousness unto Him, if we yield it as an instrument of unrighteousness unto sin? Therefore let us see to it that it is at once yielded to Him whose right it is; and let our sorrow that it should have been even for an instant desecrated to Satan's use lead us to entrust it henceforth to our Lord, to be kept by the power of God through faith for the Master's use.

For when the gentleness of Christ dwells in us, He can use the merest touch of a finger. Have we not heard of one gentle touch on a wayward shoulder being the turning point of a life? I have known a case in which the Master made use of less than that—only the quiver of a little finger being made the means of touching a wayward heart.

The Master's Touch

What must the touch of the Master's own hand have been? One imagines it very gentle, though so full of power. Can He not communicate both the power and the gentleness? When He touched the hand of Peter's mother-in-law, she arose and ministered unto them. Do you think the hand which Jesus had just touched must have ministered very excellently? As we ask Him to touch our lips with living fire, so that they may speak effectively for Him, may we not ask Him to touch our hands, that they may minister effectively, and excel in all that they find to do for Him? Then our hands shall be made strong by the hands of the mighty God of Jacob.

It is very pleasant to feel that if our hands are indeed our Lord's, we may ask Him to guide them, and strengthen them, and teach them. I do not mean figuratively, but quite literally. In everything they do for Him (and that should be *everything we ever undertake*), we want to do it well or better and better. Seek that ye may excel. We are too apt to think that He has given us certain natural gifts, but has nothing practically to do with the improvement of them, and leaves us to ourselves for that. Why not ask Him to make these hands of ours more handy for His service, more skillful in what is indicated as the next thing they are to do?

The "kept" hands need not be clumsy hands. If the Lord taught David's hands to war and his fingers to fight, will He not teach our hands, and fingers too to do what He would have them do?

The Spirit of God must have taught Bezaleel's hands as well as his head, for he was divinely empowered not only that he might devise cunning works, but also in cutting of stones and carving of timber (Ex. 31:1-5). And when all the women who were wise-hearted did spin with their hands, the hands must have been made skillful as well as the hearts made wise to prepare the beautiful garments and curtains.

There is a very remarkable instance of the hand of the Lord, which I suppose signifies in that case the power of His Spirit, being on the hand of a man. In 1 Chronicles 28:19, we read: "All this," said David, "the Lord made me understand in writing by His hand upon me, even all the works of this pattern." This cannot very well mean that the Lord gave David a miraculously written scroll, because a few verses before, it says that he had it all by the Spirit. So what else can it mean but that as David wrote, the hand of the Lord was on his hand, impelling him to trace, letter by letter, the right words of description for all the details of the temple that Solomon should build, with its courts and chambers, its treasuries and vessels? Have we not sometimes sat down to write, feeling perplexed and ignorant, and wishing someone were there to tell us what to say? At such a moment, whether it were a mere personal note or a book for publication, it is a great comfort to recollect this mighty laying of a divine hand on a human one, and ask for the same help from the same Lord. It is sure to be given!

* * * * *

And now, dear friend, what about your own hands? Are they consecrated to the Lord who loves you? And if they are, are you trusting Him to keep them, and enjoying all that is involved in that keeping? Do let this be settled with your Master before you go on to the next chapter.

After all, this question will hinge on another. Do you love Him? If you really do, there can surely be neither hesitation about yielding them to Him, nor about entrusting them to Him to be kept. *Does He love you?* That is the truer way of putting it; for it is not our love to Christ, but the love of Christ to us, which constrains us. And this is the impulse of the motion and the mode of the keeping. The steam engine does not move when the fire is not kindled, nor when it is gone out; no matter how complete the machinery and abundant the fuel, cold coals will neither set it going nor keep it working. Let us ask Him so to shed abroad His love in our hearts by the Holy Spirit which is given to us, that it may be the perpetual and only impulse of every action of our daily lives.

41

CHAPTER FOUR

OUR FEET
KEPT FOR JESUS

*"Keep my feet, that they may be
Swift and 'beautiful' for Thee."*

The figurative keeping of the feet of His saints, with the promise that when they run they shall not stumble, is a most beautiful and helpful subject. But it is quite distinct from the literal keeping for Jesus of our literal feet.

There is a certain homeliness about the idea which helps to make it very real. These very feet of ours were purchased for Christ's service by the precious drops which fell from His own torn and pierced feet on the cross. They are to be His errand-runners. How can we let the world, the flesh, and the devil have the use of what has been purchased with such payment?

Shall the world have the use of them? Shall they carry us where the world is paramount, and the Master cannot be even named, because the mention of His name would be so obviously out of place? May it never be so!

Shall the flesh have the use of them? Shall they carry us hither and thither merely because we like to go, merely because it pleases ourselves to take this walk or pay this visit? And after all, what a failure it is! If people only would believe it, self-pleasing is always a failure in the end. Our good Master gives us a reality and fullness of *pleasure* in pleasing Him which we never get out of pleasing ourselves.

Shall the devil have the use of them? Oh, no, of course not! We recoil at this seemingly unnecessary question. Yet if Jesus has not, Satan has. For as all are serving either the Prince of Life or the prince of this world, and as no man can serve two masters, it follows that if we are not serving the one, we are serving the other. And Satan is only too glad to disguise this service under the less startling form of the world, or the still less startling one of self. All that is not "kept for Jesus" is left for self or the world, and therefore for Satan.

There is no fear but that our Lord will have many uses for what is kept by Him for Himself. "How beautiful are the feet of them . . . that bring glad tidings of good things!" (Rom. 10:15) That is the best use of all; and I expect the angels think those feet beautiful, even if they are encased in muddy boots or galoshes.

Blessed Steps
Once the question was asked, "Wherefore wilt thou run, my son, seeing that thou hast no tidings ready?" (2 Sam. 18:22) So if we want to have these beautiful feet, we must have the tidings ready which they are to bear. Let us ask Him to keep our hearts so freshly full of His Good News

43

of salvation, that our mouths may speak out of their abundance. If the clouds be full of rain, they empty themselves upon the earth. May we be so filled with the Spirit that we may thus have much to pour out for others!

Besides the great privilege of carrying water from the wells of salvation, there are plenty of cups of cold water to be carried in all directions; not to the poor only—ministries of love are often as much needed by a rich friend. But the feet must be kept for these; they will be too tired for them if they are tired out from self-pleasing. In such services we are treading in the blessed steps of His most holy life, who went about doing good.

Then there is errand-going—just to fetch something that is needed for the household, or something that a tired relative wants, whether asked or unasked. Such things should come first instead of last, because these are clearly indicated as our Lord's will for us to do, by the position in which He has placed us; while what *seems* more direct service may be, after all, not so directly apportioned by Him. "I have to go and buy some soap for my mother," said a young lady with a little sigh. The sigh was a waste of breath, for her feet were going to do her Lord's will for that next half hour much more truly than if they had carried her to a Bible meeting and left the errand undone.

May it not be a comfort to those of us who feel we have not the mental or spiritual power that others have, to notice that the living sacrifice mentioned in Romans 12:1 is our "bodies"? Of course, that includes the mental power, but does it not also include the loving, sympathizing glance; the kind, encouraging word; *the ready errand for another;* the work of our hands, opportunities for all of which come more often in the day than for the mental power we are frequently tempted to envy? May we be enabled to offer willingly that which we have. "For if there be first a willing mind, it is accepted according to that a man hath, and not according to that he hath not" (2 Cor. 8:12).

If our feet are to be kept at His disposal, our eyes must be ever toward the Lord for guidance. We must look to Him for our marching orders; then He will be sure to give them. "The steps of a good man are ordered by the Lord" (Ps. 37:23). Often we find that they have been so very literally ordered for us that we are quite astonished—just as if He had not promised!

Do not smile at a *very* simple thought! If our feet are not our own, ought we not to take care of them for Him whose they are? Is it quite right to be reckless about getting wet feet, which might be guarded against, when there is, at least, a risk of hindering our service thereby? Does it please the Master when even in our zeal for His work we annoy anxious friends by carelessness in little things of this kind?

May every step of our feet be more and more like those of our beloved Master! Let us continually consider Him in this, and go where He would have gone, on the errands which He would have done, following hard after Him. And let us look on to the time when our feet shall stand in the gates of the heavenly Jerusalem, when holy feet shall tread the streets of the holy city; no longer pacing any lonely path, for He has said, "They shall walk with Me in white" (Rev. 3:4).

45

With weary human feet He, day by day,
Once trod this earth to work His acts of love;
And every step is chronicled above
His servants take to follow in His way.

CHAPTER FIVE

OUR VOICES
KEPT FOR JESUS

*"Keep my voice, that I may sing
Always, only, for my King."*

I have wondered a little at being told by a mature believer that in many cases the voice seems the last and hardest thing to yield entirely to the King; and that many who think and say they have consecrated all to the Lord and His service revolt when it comes to be a question whether they shall sing "always, only," for their King. They do not mind singing a few general sacred songs, but they do not see their way to really singing always and only unto and for Him. They want to bargain and balance a little. They question and argue about what proportion they may keep for self-pleasing and company-pleasing, and how much they must give up; and who will and who won't like it; and what they "really *must* sing," and what they "really must *not* sing" at certain times and places; and what "won't do," and what they "can't very well help," and so on.

47

And so when the question, "How much owest thou unto my Lord?" (Luke 16:15) is applied to this particularly pleasing gift, it is not met with the loyal, free-hearted, happy response, "All! Yes, *all* for Jesus!"

I know there are special temptations regarding the voice. Vain and selfish temptations whispering, "How much better a certain song suits your voice; how much more likely it is to be admired!" Faithless ones, suggesting doubts whether you can make the holy song "succeed." Deceptive ones, asking whether you ought not to please your neighbors, and ignoring the rest of the precept, "Let every one of us please his neighbor *for his good to edification*" (Rom. 15:2, italics added). Cowardly ones, telling you that it is just a little too much to expect of you, and that you are not called on to wave your banner in people's faces, and provoke surprise and remark, as this might do. And so the banner is kept furled, the witness for Jesus is not borne, and you sing for others and not for your King.

The words had passed your lips, "Take my voice!" And yet you will not let Him have it. You will not let Him have that which costs you something, just *because* it costs you something! And yet He lent you that pleasant voice that you might use it for Him. And yet He, in the sureness of His perpetual presence, was beside you all the while, and heard every note as you sang the songs which were, as your inmost heart knew, *not* for Him.

Where is your faith, your consecration? The voice has not been kept for Him because it has not been truly and unreservedly given to Him. Will you not now say: "Take my voice, for I had not given it to Thee; keep my voice, for I cannot keep it for Thee"?

48

And He will keep it! You cannot tell, till you have tried, how surely all the temptations flee when it is no longer your battle, but the Lord's; nor how completely and *curiously* all the difficulties vanish, when you simply and trustfully go forward in the path of full consecration in this matter. You will find that the keeping is most wonderfully real. Do not expect to lay down rules and provide for every sort of contingency. If you could, you would miss the sweetness of the continual guidance in the "kept" course. Have only one rule about it—just to look up to your Master about every single song you are asked or feel inclined to sing. If you are willing and obedient, you will always meet His guiding eye. He will always keep the voice that is His wholly at His disposal. Soon you will have such experience of His immediate guidance that you will be utterly satisfied with it, and only sorrowfully wonder why you did not sooner thus simply lean on it.

If you only knew, dear hesitating friends, what strength and gladness the Master gives when we loyally sing forth the honor of His name, you would not forego it! Oh, if you only knew the difficulties it saves! For when you sing "always and only for your King," you will not become entangled by the King's enemies. Singing an out-and-out sacred song often clears one's path at a stroke as to many other things. If you only knew the rewards He gives, very often then and there; the recognition that you are one of the King's friends by some lonely and timid one; the openings which you quite naturally gain of speaking a word for Jesus to hearts which, without the song, would never have given you the chance of the word! If you only

49

knew the joy of believing that His sure promise, "My Word shall not return unto Me void" (Isa. 55:11) will be fulfilled as you *sing* that word for Him! If you only tasted the solemn happiness of knowing that you have indeed a royal audience, that the King Himself is listening as you sing! If you only knew—and why should you not know? Let Him have the *whole* use of your voice at any cost, and see if He does not put many a totally unexpected new song into your mouth!

A Talent Great or Small

I am not writing all this to great and finished singers, but to everybody who can sing at all. Those who think they have only a very small talent are often most tempted not to use it for their Lord. Whether you have much or little natural voice, there is reason for its cultivation and room for its use. Place it at your Lord's disposal, and He will show you how to make the most of it for Him; for not seldom His multiplying power is brought to bear on a consecrated voice. A puzzled singing master, very famous in his profession, said to one who tried to sing for Jesus:

"Well, you have not much voice; but, mark my words, you will always outshine anybody with four times your voice!"

He was right, though he did not in the least know why.

A great many so-called sacred songs are so plaintive and pathetic that they help to give a gloomy idea of religion. Now *don't* sing these. Come out boldly, and sing definitely and unmistakably for your King, and of your King, and to your King. You will soon find, and even outsiders will have to agree, that it is a *good* thing thus to show forth His loving-kindness and His faithfulness (see Ps. 17:1-3).

Here I am usually met by the query, "But what would you advise me to sing?"

I can only say that I never got any practical help from asking anyone but the Master Himself, and so I would advise you to do the same! He knows exactly what will best suit your voice and enable you to sing best for Him; for He made it, and gave it just the pitch and tone He pleased, so of course He is the best Counselor about it. Refer your question in simplest faith to Him, and I am perfectly sure you will find it answered. He will direct you, and in some way or other the Lord will provide the right songs for you to sing.

Singing His Word

One thing I would add here: I believe there is nothing like singing His own words. The preacher claims God's promise, "My Word shall not return unto Me void" (see Isa. 55:11), and why should not the singer equally claim it? Why should not we use His own inspired words, with faith in their power, when speaking or writing, and not merely content ourselves with human words put into rhyme for our singing?

What a vista of happy work opens here! What is there to prevent our using this mightiest of all agencies committed to human agents, the Word, which is quick and powerful and sharper than any two-edged sword, whenever we are asked to sing? By this means, even a young girl may be privileged to make that Word sound in the ears of many who would not listen to it otherwise. By this the

51

incorruptible seed may be sown in otherwise unreachable ground.

For very decency's sake, a Bible song will be listened to respectfully; and for very shame's sake, no adverse whisper will be ventured against the words in ordinary homes. The singer is placed on advantageous ground, certain that at least the words of the song will be outwardly respected, and the possible ground of unfriendly criticism thus narrowed to begin with.

But there is much more than this. One feels the power of His words for one's self as one sings. One loves them and rejoices in them, and what can be greater help to any singer than that? And one knows they are true, and that they cannot really return void; and what can give greater confidence than that? God *may* bless the singing of any words, but He *must* bless the singing of His own Word, if the promise of Isaiah 55:11 means what it says.

Singing for Jesus

We must not run away with the idea that singing sacred songs and singing for Jesus are convertible terms. I know by sorrowful personal experience that it is very possible to sing a sacred song and *not* sing it for Jesus. It is easier to have one's portfolio all right than one's heart, and the repertory is more easily arranged than the motives. When we have taken our side, and the difficulties of indecision are consequently swept away, we have a new set of more subtle temptations to encounter. And although the Master will keep, the servant must watch and pray; and it is through the watching and the praying that the keeping will be effectual. We have, however, rather less excuse here than even elsewhere. For we never have to sing so very suddenly that we need to be taken unawares. This gives quite enough time for us to recollect whose we are and whom we serve, and to arouse to the watch; quite enough too for quick, trustful prayer that our singing may be kept free from that wretched self-seeking or even self-consciousness, and kept entirely for Jesus. Our best and happiest singing will flow when there is a sweet, silent undercurrent of prayerful or praiseful communion with our Master all through the song.

On the other hand, it is quite possible to sing for Jesus without singing a sacred song. Do not take a yard for the inch this seems to give, and run off with the idea that it does not matter after all what you sing, as long as you sing in a good frame of mind! No such thing! And the admission needs very careful guarding, and must not be wrested into an excuse for looking back to the world's songs. But cases may and do arise in which it may be right to gratify a weary father, or win a wayward brother, by trying to please them with music to which they will listen when they would not listen to the songs you would rather sing. There are cases in which this may be done most truly for the Lord's sake, and clearly under His guidance.

Sometimes cases arise in which we can only say, "Neither know we what to do, but our eyes are upon Thee" (2 Chron. 20:12). And when we honestly say that, we shall find the promise true, "I will guide thee with Mine eye" (Ps. 32:8). For "God is faithful, who will not suffer you to be tempted above that ye are able, but will, with the temptation, also make a way [Greek, *the* way] to escape, that ye may be able to bear it" (1 Cor. 10:13).

Remember that compromising Christians are always weak Christians. You will never be mighty to the pulling down of strongholds while you have one foot in the enemy's camp, or on the supposed neutral ground, if such can exist (which I doubt), between the camps. You will never be a terror to the devil till you have enlisted every gift and faculty on the Lord's side. Here is a thing in which you may practically carry out the splendid motto, "All for Jesus." You cannot be all for Him as long as your voice is not for Him. Which shall it be? *All* for Him, or *partly* for Him? Answer that to Him whom you call Master and Lord.

When once this question is settled, there is not much need to write in detail about other forms of singing for Jesus. As we have opportunity we shall be willing to do good with our pleasant gift in any way or place, and it is wonderful what nice opportunities He makes for us. Whether to one little sick child, or to a thousand listeners, according to the powers and openings granted, we shall take our happy position among those who minister with singing (1 Chron. 6:32). And insofar as we really do this unto the Lord, I am quite sure He gives the hundredfold now in this present time more than all the showy songs or self-gratifying performances we may have left for His sake. As we steadily tread this part of the path of conse-cration, we shall find the difficulties left behind, and the real pleasantness of the way reached, and it will be a delight to say to one's self, " I *cannot* sing the old songs"; and though you have thought it quite enough to say, "With my song will I please my friends," especially if they happened to be pleased with a mildly sacred song or two, you will strike a higher and happier, a richer and purer note, and say with David, "With my song will I praise *Him*" (Ps. 28:7, italics added). David also said, "My lips shall greatly rejoice *when* I sing unto Thee, and my soul, which Thou hast redeemed" (71:23, italics added). And you will find that this comes true.

Singing for Jesus, our Saviour and King;
Singing for Jesus, the Lord whom we love!
All adoration we joyously bring,
Longing to praise as they praise Him above.

Singing for Jesus, our Master and Friend,
Telling His love and His marvelous grace—
Love from eternity, love to the end,
Love for the loveless, the sinful, and base.

Singing for Jesus, and trying to win
Many to love Him, and join in the song,
Calling the weary and wandering in,
Rolling the chorus of gladness along.

Singing for Jesus, our Life and our Light;
Singing for Him as we press to the mark;
Singing for Him when the morning is bright;
Singing, still singing, for Him in the dark.

Singing for Jesus, our Shepherd and Guide;
Singing for gladness of heart that He gives!
Singing for wonder and praise that He died;
Singing for blessing and joy that He lives!

Singing for Jesus, oh, singing with joy;
Thus will we praise Him, and tell out His love,
Till He shall call us to brighter employ,
Singing for Jesus forever above.

CHAPTER SIX

OUR LIPS
KEPT FOR JESUS

*"Keep my lips, that they may be
Filled with messages from Thee."*

The days are past forever
when we said, "Our lips are our own." Now we know
that they are not our own.

And yet how many Christians often have the miserable
consciousness that they have spoken unadvisedly with
their lips! How many pray, "Keep the door of my lips,"
when the very last thing they think of expecting is that
they *will* be kept! They deliberately make up their minds
that hasty words, or foolish words, or exaggerated words,
according to their respective temptations, must and will
slip out of that door, and that it can't be helped. The
extent of the real meaning of their prayer was merely that
not quite so many might slip out. As their faith went no
further, the answer went no further, and so the door was
not kept. Do let us look the matter straight in the face.
Either we have committed our lips to our Lord, or we

have not. This question must be settled first. If not, oh, do not let another hour pass! Take them to Jesus, and ask Him to take them.

But when you *have* committed them to Him, it comes to this—is He able or is He not able to keep that which you have committed to Him? If He is not able, of course you may as well give up at once, for your own experience has abundantly proved that *you* are not able, so there is no help for you. But if He is able—nay, thank God, there is no *if* on this side—say, rather, *as* He is able, where was this inevitable necessity of perpetual failure? You have been fancying yourself virtually doomed and fated to it, and therefore you have gone on in it, while all the time His arm was not shortened that it could not save, but you have been limiting the Holy One of Israel. Honestly now, have you trusted Him to keep your lips *this day?* Trust necessarily implies expectation that what we have entrusted will be kept. If you have not expected Him to keep, you have not trusted. You may have tried, and tried very hard, but you have not *trusted,* and therefore you have not been kept, and your lips have been the snare of your soul (see Prov. 18:7).

Once I heard a beautiful prayer which I can never forget; it was this:

"Lord, take my lips, and speak through them; take my mind, and think through it; take my heart, and set it on fire."

And this is the way the Master keeps the lips of His servants, by so filling their hearts with His love that the outflow cannot be unloving, by so filling their thoughts that the utterance cannot be un-Christlike. There must be filling before there *can* be pouring out; and if there is filling, there *must* be pouring out, for He has said, "Out of the abundance of the heart the mouth speaketh" (Matt. 12:34).

But I think we should look for something more direct and definite than this. We are not all called to be the King's ambassadors, but *all* who have heard the message of salvation for themselves are called to be the Lord's messengers, and day by day, as He gives us opportunity, we are to deliver "the Lord's message unto the people." That message, as committed to Haggai, was " 'I am with you,' saith the Lord" (Hag. 1:13). Is there not work enough for any lifetime in unfolding and distributing that one message to His own people? Then, for those who are still far off, we have that equally full message from our Lord to give out, which He has condensed for us into the one word, "Come!"

It is a specially sweet part of His dealings with His messengers that He always gives us the message for ourselves first. It is what He has first told us in darkness— that is, in the secrecy of our own rooms, or at least of our own hearts—that He bids us speak in light. And so the more we sit at His feet and watch to see what He has to say to us, the more we shall have to tell to others. He does not send us out with sealed dispatches, which we know nothing about, and with which we have no concern.

There seems a sevenfold sequence in His filling the lips of His messengers. (1) They must be purified. The live coal from the altar must be laid on them, and He must say, "Lo, this hath touched thy lips, and thine iniquity is taken away, and thy sin is purged" (Isa. 6:7). (2) Then He will create the fruit of them, and this seems to be the great message of peace. " 'Peace to him that is far off and to him that is near,' saith the Lord; 'and I will heal him' " (57:19). (3) Then comes the prayer, "O Lord, open Thou my lips" (Ps. 51:15) and its sure fulfillment. (4) Then come the promises, "Behold, I have put My words in thy mouth" (Isa. 51:16) and, "They shall withal be fitted in thy lips" (Prov. 22:18). (5) Then, of course, "the lips of the righteous feed many" (10:21) for the food is the Lord's own giving. (6) Everything leads up to praise, and so we come next to, "My mouth shall praise Thee with joyful lips, when I remember Thee" (Ps. 63:5). (7) And lest we should fancy that *when* rather implies that it is not, or cannot be, exactly *always*, we find that the meditation of Jesus throws this added light upon it, "by *Him*, therefore, let us offer the sacrifice of praise to God *continually*, that is, the fruit of our lips, giving thanks to [margin, confessing] His name" (Heb. 13:15, italics added).

Does it seem a coming down from the mount to glance at one of our King's commandments, which is specially needful and applicable to this matter of our lips being kept for Him? "Watch and pray, that ye enter not into temptation" (Matt. 26:41). None of His commands clash with or supersede another. Trusting does not supersede watching; it does but complete and effectuate it. Unwatchful trust is a delusion, and untrustful watching is in vain. Therefore let us not either willfully or carelessly *enter* into temptation, whether of place, or person, or topic, which has any tendency to endanger the keeping of our lips for Jesus. Let us pray that grace may be more and more poured into our lips as it was into His lips, so that our speech may be *always* with grace. May they be pure, and sweet, and lovely, even as "His lips, like lilies, dropping sweet-smelling myrrh" (Song 5:13).

The Power of Influence

We can hardly consider the keeping of our lips without recollecting that upon them, more than all else (though not exclusively of all else), depends that greatest of our responsibilities, our influence. We have no choice in the matter; we cannot evade or avoid it; and there is no more possibility of our limiting it, or even tracing its limits, than there is of setting a bound to the far-vibrating sound waves, or watching their flow through the invisible air. Every sentence that passes our lips is an invisibly prolonged influence, not dying away into silence, but living away into the words and deeds of others.

We all know that there is influence exerted by a person's mere presence, without the utterance of a single word. We are conscious of this every day. People seem to carry an atmosphere with them, which *must* be breathed by those whom they approach. Some carry an atmosphere in which all unkind thoughts shrivel up and cannot grow into expression. Others carry one in which thoughts of Christ and things divine never seem able to flourish. Have you not felt how a happy conversation about the things we love best is checked, or even strangled, by the entrance of one who is not in sympathy? Outsiders never have a chance of really knowing what delightful intercourse we have with one another about these things, because their very presence chills and changes it. On the other hand, how another person's incoming freshens and develops it and warms us all up, and seems to give us, without the least conscious effort, a sort of *lift!*

If even unconscious and involuntary influence is such a power, how much greater must it be when the recognized power of words is added!

It has often struck me as a matter of observation that open profession of Jesus Christ adds force to this influence, on whichever side it weighs; and also that it has the effect of making many a word and act, which might in other hands have been as nearly neutral as anything can be, tell with by no means neutral tendency on the wrong side. The question of Eliphaz comes with great force when applied to one who desires or professes to be consecrated altogether, life *and* lips: "Should *he* reason with unprofitable talk and with speeches *wherewith one can do no good?*" (Job 15:3, italics added) There is our standard! Idle words, which might have fallen comparatively harmlessly from one who had never named the name of Christ, may be a stumbling block to inquirers, a sanction to thoughtless juniors, and a grief to thoughtful seniors, when they come from the lips which are professing to feed many. Even intelligent talk on general subjects by such a one may be a chilling disappointment to some craving heart, which had indulged the hope of getting help, comfort, or instruction in the things of God by listening to the conversation. It may be a lost opportunity of giving and gaining no one knows *how* much!

How well I recollect this disappointment to myself, again and again, when a mere child! In those early seeking days I never could understand why, sometimes, a good man whom I heard preach or speak as if he loved

Christ very much talked about all sorts of other things
when we came back from church or missionary meeting. I
did so wish he would have talked about the Saviour,
whom I wanted, but had not found. It would have been
so much more interesting even to the apparently thoughtless and merry little girl. How could he help it, I wondered, if he cared for that pearl of great price as I was sure
I should care for it if I could only find it! And oh, why
didn't these pastors ever talk to me about it, instead of
about my lessons or their little girls at home? They did not
know how their conversation was observed and compared with their sermon or speech, and how a hungry
little soul went away empty from the supper table.

The lips of younger Christians may cause, in their turn,
no less disappointment. One sorrowful lesson I can never
forget; and I will tell the story in hope that it may save
others from causes of similar regret. During a summer
visit just after I had left school, a class of girls about my
own age came to me a few times for an hour's singing. It
was very pleasant indeed, and the girls were delighted
with the hymns. They listened to all I had to say about
time and expression, and not with less attention to the
more shyly ventured remarks about the words. Sometimes I accompanied them afterward down the avenue;
and whenever I met any of them I had smiles and plenty
of kindly words for each, which they seemed to appreci-
ate immensely. A few years afterward I sat by the bedside
of one of these girls—the most gifted of them all with both
heart and head. She had been led by a wonderful way,
and through long and deep suffering, into far clearer light
than I enjoyed, and had witnessed for Christ in more

63

ways than one, and far more brightly than I had ever done. She told me how sorrowfully and eagerly she was seeking Jesus at the time of those singing classes. And I never knew it, because I never asked, and she was too shy to speak first! But she told me more, and every word was a pang to me—how she used to linger in the avenue on those summer evenings, longing that I would speak to her about the Saviour; how she hoped, week after week, that I would just stretch out a hand to help her, just say one little word that might be God's message of peace to her, instead of the pleasant, general remarks about the nice hymns and tunes. And I never did! And she went on for months, I think for years, after, without the light and gladness which it might have been my privilege to bring to her life. God chose others means, for the souls that He has given to Christ cannot be lost because of the unfaithfulness of a human instrument. But she said, and the words often ring in my ears when I am tempted to let an opportunity slip:

"Ah, Miss Frances, I ought to have been *yours!*"

A Call to Witness

Yes, it is true enough that we should show forth His praise not only with our lips, but in our lives; but with very many Christians the other side of the prayer wants praying—they want rousing up even to *wish* to show it forth not only in their lives, but with their lips. I wonder how many, even of those who read this, really pray, "O Lord, open Thou *my* lips, and my mouth shall show forth Thy praise!" (Ps. 51:15, italics added)

And when opened, oh, how much one *does* want to

have them so kept for Jesus that He may be free to make the most of them, not letting them render second-rate and indirect service when they might be doing direct and first-rate service to His cause and kingdom! It is terrible how much less is done for Him than *might* be done, in consequence of the deceptive notion that if what we are doing or saying is not bad, we are doing good in a certain way, and therefore may be quite easy about it. People are not converted by this sort of work; at any rate *I* never met or heard of anyone. "He thinks it better for his quiet influence to tell!" said an affectionately excusing relative of one who had plenty of special opportunities of soul-winning, if he had only used his lips as well as his life for His Master. "And how many souls have been converted to God by his quiet influence all these years?" was my reply. And to that there was no answer! For the silent shining was all very beautiful in theory, but not one of the many souls placed specially under his influence had been known to be brought out of darkness into marvelous light. If they had, it would have been obvious for such light can't help being seen.

When one has even a glimmer of the tremendous difference between having Christ and being without Christ; when one gets but one shuddering glimpse of what eternity is, and of what it must mean, as well as what it may mean, without Christ; when one gets but a flash of realization of the tremendous fact that all these neighbors of ours, rich and poor alike, will *have* to spend that eternity either with Him or without Him—it is hard, very hard, indeed, to understand how a man or woman can believe these things at all, and make no effort for anything beyond the temporal elevation of those around, sometimes not even beyond their amusements! "People must have entertainment," they urge. I do not find that *must* in the Bible, but I do find, "We *must* all appear before the Judgment Seat of Christ" (2 Cor. 5:10, italics added). And if you have any sort of belief in that, how can you care to use those lips of yours, which might be a fountain of life to the dying souls before you, merely to entertain them at some entertainment? As you sow, so you reap. The amusing paper is read, or the lively ballad recited, or the popular song sung, and you reap your harvest of laughter or applause, and of complacence at your success in entertaining people. And there it ends, when you might have sown words from which you and they should reap fruit unto life eternal. Is this worthy work for one who has been bought with such a price that he must say,

> Love so amazing, so divine,
> Demands my soul, my life, my all?

So far from yielding "all" to that rightful demand of amazing love, he does not even yield the fruit of his lips to it, much less the lips themselves.

After all, nothing really pays like direct, straightforward, uncompromising words about God and His works and Word. Nothing else ever made a man say, as a poor Irishman did when he heard the Good News for the first time:

"Thank ye, kind sir; you've taken the hunger off us today!"

The Need for Self-examination

Bearing in mind that it is not only the words which pass their lightly hinged portal, but our literal lips which are to be kept for Jesus, it cannot be out of place before closing this chapter to suggest that they open both ways. What passes in should surely be considered as well as what passes out. And very many of us are beginning to see that the command, "Whether ye eat or drink or whatsoever ye do, do all to the glory of God" (1 Cor. 10:31) is not fully obeyed when we drink liquor, merely because we like it. What matter that we prefer taking it in a more refined form, if the thing itself is daily and actively and mightily working misery, and crime, and death, and destruction to thousands, till the cry thereof seems as if it must pierce the very heavens! And so it does—sooner, a great deal, than it pierces the walls of our comfortable dining rooms! I only say here, to you who have said, "Take my lips," stop and repeat that prayer next time you put that to your lips which is binding men and women, hand and foot, and delivering them over, helpless, to Satan! Let those words pass once more from your heart *out* through your lips and I do not think you will feel comfortable in letting the means of such infernal work pass *in* through them.

CHAPTER SEVEN

OUR SILVER AND GOLD KEPT FOR JESUS

*"Keep my silver and my gold;
Not a mite would I withhold."*

"'T**he silver is Mine, and the gold is Mine,' saith the Lord of hosts" (Hag. 2:8). Yes, every coin we have is literally our Lord's money. Simple belief of this fact is the stepping-stone to full consecration of what He has given us, whether much or little.

"Then you mean to say we are never to spend anything on ourselves?" Not so. Another fact must be considered— the fact that our Lord has given us our bodies as a special personal charge, and that we are responsible for keeping these bodies, according to the means given and the work required, in working order for Him. This is part of our "own work." A master entrusts a work-man with a delicate machine, with which his appointed work is to be done. He also provides him with a sum of money with which he is to procure all that may be necessary for keeping the machine in thorough repair.

Is it not obvious that it is the man's distinct duty to see to this faithfully? Would he not be failing in duty if he chose to spend it all on something for somebody else's work, or on a present for his master, fancying that would please him better, while the machine is creaking and wearing for want of a little oil, or working badly for want of a new band or screw? Just so, we are to spend what is really needful *on* ourselves, because it is our charge to do so; but not *for* ourselves, because we are not our own, but our Master's. He who knows our frame knows its need of rest and medicine, food and clothing; and the procuring of these for our own entrusted bodies should be done just as much "for Jesus" as the greater pleasure of procuring them for someone else. Therefore, there need be no quibbling over the assertion that consecration is not real and complete while we are looking upon a single shilling as our own to do with what we like. Also the principle is exactly the same, whether we are spending pence or pounds; it is our Lord's money, and must not be spent without reference to Him.

When we have asked Him to take and continually trust Him to keep our money, we look up to our Lord for guidance to lay out His money prudently and rightly, and as He would have us lay it out. The gift or garment is selected consciously under His eye, and with conscious reference to Him as our own dear Master, for whose sake we shall give it, or in whose service we shall wear it, and with whose own silver or gold we shall pay for it, and then it is all right.

But have you found out that one of the Lord's secrets is that when any of His dear children turn aside a little bit after having once entered the blessed path of truth and conscious consecration, He is sure to send them some little punishment? He will not let us go back without a sharp, even if quite secret, reminder. Go and spend ever such a little without reference to Him after you have pledged the silver and gold entirely to Him, and see if you are not in some way rebuked for it! Very often by being permitted to find that you have made a mistake in your purchase, or that in some way it does not prosper. If you "observe these things," you will find that the more closely we are walking with our Lord, the more immediate and unmistakable will be His gracious rebukes when we swerve in any detail of the full consecration to which He has called us. And if you have already experienced and recognized this part of His personal dealing with us, you will know also how we love and bless Him for it.

Tithes and Firstfruits

There is always a danger that just because we say "all" we may practically fall shorter than if we had only said "some," but said it very definitely. God recognizes this and provides against it in many departments.

For instance, though our time is to be "all" for Him, yet He solemnly sets apart one day in seven which is to be specially for Him. Those who think they know better than God, and profess that every day is a Sabbath, little know what floodgates of temptation they are opening by being so very wise above what is written. God knows best, and that should be quite enough for every loyal heart.

So, as to money, though we place it all at our Lord's disposal, and rejoice to spend it all for Him directly or indirectly, yet I am quite certain it is a great help and safeguard and what is more, a matter of simple obedience to the spirit of His commands, to set aside a definite and regular proportion of our income or receipts for His direct service. It is a great mistake to suppose that the law of giving the tenth to God is merely levitical. Search and look for yourselves, and you will find it is, like the Sabbath, a far older rule, running all through the Bible and endorsed, not abrogated, by Christ Himself. (See Gen. 14:20; 28:22; Lev. 27:30, 32; Num. 18:21; Deut. 14:22; 2 Chron. 31:5-6, 12; Neh. 10:37; 12:44; 13:12; Mal. 3:8, 10; 1 Cor. 16:2; Heb. 7:8.) For speaking of tithes, He said, "These *ought* ye to have done, and not to leave the other undone" (Matt. 23:23; Luke 11:42, italics added). To dedicate the tenth of whatever we have is mere duty. Charity begins beyond it. Freewill offerings and thank offerings beyond that again.

Firstfruits, also, should be thus specially set apart. This too we find running all through the Bible. There is a tacit appeal to our gratitude in the suggestion of them—the very word implies bounty received and bounty in prospect. Bringing "the first of the firstfruits into the house of the Lord" was like "saying grace" for all the plenty He was going to bestow on the faithful Israelite. Something of gladness too seems always implied. "The day of the firstfruits" was to be a day of rejoicing (compare Num. 28:26 with Deut. 16:10-11). There is also an appeal to loyalty: we are commanded to *honor* the Lord with the firstfruits of all our increase. And *that* is the way to prosper, for the next word is, "*So* shall thy barns be filled with plenty" (Prov. 3:9-10, italics added). The friend who first called my attention to this command said that setting apart firstfruits—making a proportion for God's work a first *charge* upon the income—always seemed to bring a blessing on the rest, and that since this had been systematically done, it actually seemed to go further than when not thus lessened.

Presenting our firstfruits should be a peculiarly delightful act, as they are themselves the emblem of our consecrated relationship to God. "For of His own will begat He us with the Word of truth, that we should be a kind of firstfruits of His creatures" (James 1:18). How sweet and hallowed and richly emblematic our little acts of obedience in this matter become when we throw this light upon them! And how blessedly they may remind us of the heavenly company, singing (as it were) a new song before the throne; for they are the firstfruits unto God and to the Lamb.

Perhaps we shall find no better plan of detailed and systematic setting apart than the New Testament one: "Upon the first day of the week let every one of you lay by him in store, as God hath prospered him" (1 Cor. 16:2). The very act of literally fulfilling this apostolic command seems to bring a blessing with it as all simple obedience does. I wish, dear friends, you would try it! You will find it a sweet reminder on His own day of this part of your consecration. You will find it an immense help in making the most of your little charities. The regular inflow will guide the outflow and ensure your always having *something* for any sudden call for your Master's poor or your Master's cause.

Do not say you are afraid you could not keep to it. What

has a consecrated life to do with being afraid? Some of us could tell of such sweet and singular lessons of trust in this matter that they are written in golden letters of love on our memories. Of course, there will be trials of our faith in this, as well as in everything else. But every trial of our faith is but a trial of His faithfulness, and is much more precious than gold which perishes (1 Peter 1:7).

Self-denial and Self-delight

"What about self-denial?" some reader will say. Consecration does not supersede this, but transfigures it. Literally, a consecrated life is and must be a life of denial of self. But all the effort and pain of it is changed into very delight. We love our Master; we know, surely and absolutely, that He is listening and watching our every word and way, and that He has called us to the privilege of walking worthy of the Lord unto all pleasing (see Col. 1:10). And insofar as this is a reality to us, the identical things which are still self-*denial* in one sense become actual self-*delight* in another. It may be self-denial to us to turn away from something within reach of our purse that would be very convenient or pleasant to possess; but if the Master lifted the veil and revealed Himself standing at our side, and let us hear His audible voice asking us to reserve the price of it for His treasury, should we talk about self-denial then? Should we not be utterly ashamed to think of it? Or rather, should we, for one instant, think about self or self-denial at all? Would it not be an unimaginable joy to do what He asked us to do with that money? But as long as His own unchangeable promise stands written in His Word for us, "Lo, I am with you *alway*"

73

(Matt. 28:20, italics added), we may be sure that He *is* with us, and that His eye is as certainly on our opened or half-opened purse as it was on the treasury when He sat over against it and saw the two mites cast in. So let us do our shopping as seeing Him who is invisible.

It is important to remember that there is no much or little in God's sight except as relative to our means and willingness. "For if there be first a willing mind, it is accepted according to that a man hath, and not according to that he hath not" (2 Cor. 8:12). He knows what we have *not* as well as what we have. He knows all about the low wages in one sphere, and the small allowance, or the fixed income with rising prices in another. And it is not a question of paying to God what can be squeezed out of these, but of giving Him all, then holding all at His disposal, and taking His orders about the disposal of all.

But I do not see at all how self-indulgence and needless extravagance can possibly coexist with true consecration. If we really never *go without* anything for the Lord's sake, but, just because He has graciously given us means, always supply for ourselves not only every need but every notion, I think it is high time we looked into the matter before God. Why should only those who have limited means have the privilege of offering to their Lord that which has really cost them something to offer? Observe, it is not *merely* going without something we would naturally like to have or do, but going without it *for Jesus' sake*. Not, "I will go without it because, after all, I can't very well afford it"; or "because I really ought to subscribe to So-and-so"; or "because I daresay I shall be glad I have not spent the money": but "I will do without it because I *do*

74

want to do a little more for Him who so loves me—just that much more than I could do if I did this other thing." I fancy this is more often the heart-language of those who *have* to cut and contrive than of those who are able to give liberally without any cutting and contriving at all. The very abundance of God's gifts too often hinders from the privilege and delight of really doing without something superfluous or comfortable or usual, that they may give just that much more to their Lord. What a pity!

Someone has aptly written, "Simplicity in all habits of life should be a mark of the followers of Him who had nowhere to lay His head. . . . The self-indulgence of wealthy Christians, who might largely support the Lord's work with what they lavish upon their houses, their tables, or their personal expenditures, is very sad to see."

On the other hand, it is very possible to be fairly faithful in much and yet unfaithful in that which is least. We may have thought about our gold and silver, and yet have been altogether thoughtless about our rubbish! Some have a habit of hoarding away old garments, pieces, remnants, and odds and ends generally under the idea that they will come in useful someday; very likely setting it up as a kind of mild virtue, backed by that noxious old saying, "Keep it by you seven years, and you'll find a use for it." And so the shabby things get shabbier, and moth and dust corrupt, and the drawers and places get choked and crowded; and meanwhile all this that is sheer rubbish to you might be made useful at once, to a degree beyond what you would guess, to some poor person. Indeed, there are hundreds of poor missionaries' families to whom a few old garments or any household items are as great a charity as to any of the poor under their charge.

* * * * *

There is no bondage in consecration. The two things are opposites and cannot coexist, much less mingle. We should suspect our consecration and come afresh to our great Counselor about it the moment we have any sense of bondage. As long as we have an unacknowledged feeling of fidget about our account book, and a smothered wondering what and how much we *ought* to give, and a hushed-up wishing the thing had not been put quite so strongly before us, we can be certain we have not said unreservedly, "Take my silver and my gold." And how can the Lord keep what He has not been sincerely asked to take?

Ah! If we had stood at the foot of the cross, and watched the tremendous payment of our redemption with the precious blood of Christ—if we had seen that awful price tolled out, drop by drop, from His own dear patient brow and torn hands and feet, till it was ALL paid, and the central word of eternity was uttered, *"It is finished!"* should we not have been ready to say, *"Not a mite will I withhold"*?

CHAPTER EIGHT

OUR INTELLECTS KEPT FOR JESUS

*"Keep my intellect, and use
Every power as Thou shalt choose."*

There are two distinct sets of temptations which assail those who have, or think they have, rather less, and those who have, or think they have, rather more than an average share of intellect; while those who have neither less nor more are generally open in some degree to both. The refuge and very present help from both is the same. The intellect, whether great or small, which is committed to the Lord's keeping, will be kept and will be used by Him.

No Grounds for Excuse

The former class are tempted to think themselves excused from effort to cultivate and use their small intellectual gifts; to suppose they cannot or need not seek to win souls because they are not so clever and apt in speech as So-and-so; to attribute to want of spiritual gifts what is really want of grace; to hide the one talent because it is not five. Let me throw out a thought or two for these.

Which is greatest, gifts or grace? *Gifts* are given to every man according to his abilities. That is, we have just as much given as God knows we are able to use, and what He knows we can best use, for Him. "But unto every one of us is given *grace* according to the measure of the gift of Christ" (Eph. 4:7, italics added). Claiming and using that royal measure of grace, you may, and can, and will do more for God than the mightiest intellect in the world without it. For which, in the clear light of His Word, is likely to be most effectual, the natural ability which at its best and fullest, without Christ, can do *nothing* (observe and believe that word!), or the grace of our Almighty God and the power of the Holy Spirit which is as free to you as it ever was to anyone?

If you are responsible for making use of your limited gift, are you not equally responsible for making use of the grace and power which are to be had for the asking, which are already yours in Christ, and which are not limited?

Also, do you not see that when there are great natural gifts, people give the credit to *them*, instead of to the grace which alone did the real work, and thus God is defrauded of the glory? So that, to say it reverently, God can get more glory out of a feeble instrument, because then it is more obvious that the excellency of the power is of God and not of us. Will you not henceforth say, "Most gladly therefore, will I rather glory in my infirmities, that the power of Christ may rest upon me"? (2 Cor. 12:9)

Don't you really believe that the Holy Spirit is just as

OUR INTELLECTS KEPT FOR JESUS

able to draw a soul to Jesus, if He will, by your whisper of the one word *"Come,"* as by an eloquent sermon an hour long? *I* do! At the same time, as it is evidently God's way to work through these intellects of ours, we have no more right to expect Him to use a mind which we are willfully neglecting, and taking no pains whatever to fit for His use, than I should have to expect you to write a beautiful inscription with my pen, if I would not take the trouble to fill it with ink.

No Grounds for Pride

The latter class are tempted to rely on their natural gifts, and to act and speak in their own strength; to go on too fast, without really looking up at every step, and for every word; to spend their Lord's time in polishing up their intellects, nominally for the sake of influence and power, and so forth, while really, down at the bottom, it is for the sake of the keen enjoyment of the process; and perhaps, most of all, to spend the strength of these intellects for that which doesn't profit, in yielding to the deceptive snare of reading clever books on both sides, and eating deliberately of the tree of knowledge of good *and evil*.

The mere mention of these temptations should be sufficient appeal to conscience. If consecration is to be a reality anywhere, should it not be in the very thing which you own as an extra gift from God, and which is evidently closest, so to speak, to His direct action, spirit upon spirit? And if the very strength of your intellect has been your weakness, will you not entreat Him to keep it henceforth really and entirely for Himself? It is so good of Him to have given you something to lay at His feet; shall not this goodness lead you to lay it *all* there, and never hanker after taking it back for yourself or the world? Do you not feel that in equal proportion to the gift, you need the special keeping of it? He may lead you by a way you know not in the matter. Very likely He will show you that you must be willing to be a fool for His sake first, before He will condescend to use you much for His glory. Will you look up into His face and say, *"Not* willing"?

The Maker of the Mind

He who made every power can use every power—memory, judgment, imagination, quickness of apprehension or insight; specialties of musical, poetical, oratorical, or artistic faculty; special tastes for reasoning, philosophy, history, natural science, or natural history—all these may be dedicated to Him, sanctified by Him, and used by Him. Whatever He has given, He will use, if we will let Him. Often, in the most unexpected ways, and at the most unexpected turns, something read or acquired long ago suddenly comes into use. We cannot foresee what will thus be useful; but He knew, when He guided us to learn it, what it would be wanted for in His service. So may we not ask Him to bring His perfect foreknowledge to bear on all our mental training and storing? To guide us to read or study exactly what He knows there will be use for in the work to which He has called or will call us?

Nothing is more practically perplexing to a young Christian, whose preparation time is not quite over, or perhaps painfully limited, than to know what is most worth studying, what is really the best investment of the golden hours, while yet the time is not come for the field of active work to be fully entered, and the thorough furnishing of the mind is the evident path of present duty. Is not His name called "Counselor"? And will He not be faithful to the promise of His name in this, as well as in all else?

The same applies to every subsequent stage. Only let us be perfectly clear about the principle that our intellect is not our own, either to cultivate, or to use, or to enjoy, and that Jesus Christ is our real and ever-present Counselor, and then there will be no more worry about what to read and how much to read, and whether to keep up one's accomplishments, or one's languages, or one's *ologies!* If the Master has need of them, He will show us; and if He has not, what need have we of them? If we go forward without His leading, we may throw away some talent, or let it get too rusty for use, which would have been most valuable when other circumstances arose or different work was given. We must not think that "keeping" means not using at all! What we want is to have all our powers kept for His *use.* When we do we will find far higher development than in any other sort of use. I know cases in which the effect of real consecration on mere mental development has been obvious and surprising to all around. Yet it is only a confirmation of what I believe to be a great principle: *the Lord makes the most of whatever is unreservedly surrendered to Him.* There will always be plenty of waste in what we try to cut out for ourselves. But He wastes no material!

CHAPTER NINE

OUR WILLS
KEPT FOR JESUS

"Keep my will, O keep it Thine;
For it is no longer mine."

Perhaps there is no point in which expectation has been so limited by experience as this. We believe God is able to do for us just so much as He has already done, and no more. We take it for granted a line must be drawn somewhere; and so we choose to draw it where experience ends, and faith would have to begin. Even if we have trusted and proved Him as to keeping our bodies and our minds, faith fails when we would go deeper and say, "Keep my will!" And yet the only reason we have to give is that though we have asked Him to take our wills, we do not exactly find that they are altogether His, but that self-will crops up again and again. And whatever flaw there might be in this argument we think the matter is quite settled by the fact that some whom we rightly esteem, and who are far better than ourselves, have the same experience, and do not even seem to think it right to hope for anything better. That is conclusive! And the result of this, as of every other faith-less conclusion, is either discouragement and depression, or, still worse, acquiescence to an unyielded will, as something that can't be helped.

God's Will or Ours?

Now let us turn from our thoughts to God's thoughts. Truly, they are not as ours! He says He is able to do exceeding abundantly above all that we ask or think (see Eph. 3:20). Apply this here.

We ask Him to take our wills and make them His. Does He or does He not mean what He says? And if He does, should we not trust Him to do this thing that we have asked and longed for, and not less, but more? Is *anything* too hard for the Lord? Has He said, and shall He not do it? And if He gives us faith to believe that we have the petition that we desired of Him, and with it the unspeakable rest of leaning our will wholly upon His love, what ground have we for imagining that this is *necessarily* to be a mere fleeting shadow, which is hardly to last an hour, but is *necessarily* to be exhausted ere the next breath of trial or temptation comes? Does He mock our longing by acting as I have seen an older person act to a child, by accepting some trifling gift of no intrinsic value, just to please the little one, and then throwing it away as soon as the child's attention is diverted? Is not the taking rather the pledge of the keeping, if we will but entrust Him fearlessly with it? We give Him no opportunity (so to speak) of proving His faithfulness to this great promise because we *will* not fulfill the condition of reception, believing it. But we readily enough believe instead all that we hear of the unsatisfactory experience of others!

It may be that we have not sufficiently realized the sin of the only alternative. Our wills belong either to self or to God. It may seem a small and rather excusable sin in man's sight to be self-willed, but in what a category of iniquity God puts it! (2 Peter 2:10) And certainly we are without excuse when we have such a promise to go upon as, "It is God that worketh in you both to *will* and to do of His good pleasure" (Phil. 2:13, italics added). How splendidly this meets our very deepest helplessness—"works in you to *will*"! Oh, let us pray for ourselves and for each other that we may know "what is the exceeding greatness of His power to usward who believe" (Eph. 1:19). It does not say, "to usward who fear and doubt"; for if we will not believe, neither shall we be established. If we will not believe what God says He can do, we shall see it with our eyes but we shall not eat thereof. "They *could* not enter in because of unbelief" (Heb. 3:19, italics added).

It is most comforting to remember that the grand promise, "Thy people shall be willing in the day of Thy power" (Ps. 110:3), is made by the Father to Christ Himself. The Lord Jesus holds this promise, and God will fulfill it to Him. He will make us willing because He has promised Jesus that He will do so. And what is being made willing, but having our wills taken and kept?

True Surrender

All true surrender of the will is based on love and knowledge of, and confidence in, the one to whom it is surrendered. We have the human analogy so often before our eyes, that it is the more strange we should be so slow to own even the possibility of it as to God. Is it thought anything so very extraordinary and high-flown when a bride deliberately *prefers* wearing a color which was not her own taste or choice, because her husband likes to see her in it? Is it very unnatural that it is no distress to her to do what he asks her to do, or to go with him where he asks her to go, even without question or explanation, instead of doing what or going where she would undoubtedly have preferred if she did not know and love him? Is it very surprising if this lasts beyond the wedding day, and if year after year she still finds it her greatest pleasure to please him, quite irrespective of what *used* to be her own ways and likings? Yet in this case she is not helped by any promise or power on his part to make her wish what he wishes. But He who so wonderfully condescends to call Himself the Bridegroom of His church, and who claims our fullest love and trust, has promised and has power to work in us to will. Shall we not claim His promise and rely on His mighty power, and say, not self-confidently, but looking only unto Jesus—

Keep my will, for it is Thine;
It shall be no longer mine!

Only in proportion as our own will is surrendered are we able to discern the splendor of God's will.

Conversely, in proportion as we see this splendor of His will, we shall more readily or more fully surrender our own. Not until we have presented our bodies as living sacrifices can we prove what is that good, and perfect, and acceptable will of God (see Rom. 12:1-2). But in thus proving it, this continual presentation will be more and more seen to be our reasonable service, and become more and more a joyful sacrifice of praise.

Sustaining Love

The connection in Romans 12:1-2 between our sacrifice which He so graciously calls acceptable to Himself, and our finding out that His will is acceptable to ourselves, is very striking. One reason for this connection may be that only love can really understand love, and love on both sides is at the bottom of the whole transaction and its results. First, He loves us. Then the discovery of this leads us to love Him. Then, because He loves us, He claims us, and desires to have us wholly yielded to His will, so that the operations of love in and for us may find no hindrance. Then, because we love Him we recognize His claim and yield ourselves. Then, being thus yielded, He draws us nearer to Him (2 Chron. 29:31), and admits us (so to speak) into closer intimacy, so that we gain nearer and truer views of His perfections. Then, the unity of these perfections becomes clearer to us. Now we not only see His justice and mercy flowing in an undivided stream from the Cross of Christ, but we see that they never were divided, though the strange distortions of the dark, false glass of sin made them appear so; both are but emanations of God's holy love. Then having known and believed this holy love, we see further that His will is not a separate thing, but only love (and therefore all His attributes) in action; love being the primary essence of His being, and all the other attributes merely manifestations and combinations of that ineffable essence, for God *is* love. Then this will of God, which has seemed in old far-off days a stern and fateful power, is seen to be only love energized; love saying, "I will." And when once we really grasp this (hardly so much by faith as by love itself), the will of God cannot be otherwise than acceptable, for it is no longer a question of trusting that somehow or other there is a hidden element of love in it, but of understanding that it *is* love; no more to be dissociated from it than the power of the sun's rays can be dissociated from their light and warmth. And love recognized must surely be love accepted and reciprocated. So, as the fancied sternness of God's will is lost in His love, the stubbornness of our wills becomes melted in that love, and lost in our acceptance of it.

CHAPTER TEN

OUR HEARTS
KEPT FOR JESUS

"Keep my heart; it is Thine own;
It is now Thy royal throne."

I t is a good thing that the
heart be established with grace, and yet some of us
go on as if it were not a good thing even to hope for
it to be so.

We should be ashamed to say that we had behaved
treacherously to a friend; that we had played him false
again and again; that we had said scores of times what we
did not really mean; that we had professed and promised
what, all the while, we had no intention of performing.
We should be ready to go off by the next ship to some
remote island rather than calmly admit to all this, or
rather than ever face our friend again after we had admit-
ted it. And yet we are not ashamed (some of us) to say
that we are always dealing treacherously with our Lord:
nay more, we admit it with an inexplicable complacency,
as if there were a kind of virtue in saying how fickle and

faithless and desperately wicked our hearts are; and we actually pride ourselves on the easy confession, which we think proves our humility, and which does not lower us in the eyes of others, nor in our own eyes, half so much as if we had to say, "I have told a lie," or, "I have broken my promise." Nay, more, we have not the slightest hope, and therefore not the smallest intention, of aiming at an utterly different state of things. Well for us if we do not go a step further, and call those by hard and false names who do seek to have an established heart, and who believe that as the Lord meant what He said when He promised, *"No good thing will He withhold from them that walk uprightly"* (Ps. 84:11, italics added), so He will not withhold *this* good thing.

Prayer must be based on promise, but, thank God, His promises are always broader than our prayers! No fear of building inverted pyramids here, for Jesus Christ is the foundation, and this and all the other promises of God in Him are yes, and in Him Amen, unto the glory of God by us (see 2 Cor. 1:20). So it shall be unto His glory to fulfill this one to us, and to answer our prayer for a "kept" or "established" heart. And its fulfillment shall work out His glory, not in spite of us, but *by* us.

A Heart Fixed on God

We find both the means and the result of the keeping in Psalm 112: "His heart is fixed" (v. 7). Whose heart? An angel's? A saint's in glory? No! Simply the heart of the man who fears the Lord, and delights greatly in His commandments (v. 1). Therefore yours and mine, as God would have them be; just the normal idea of a God-fearing heart, nothing hopelessly beyond reach.

Fixed! How does that compare with the deceitfulness and waywardness and fickleness we so often display as if we were proud of our faltering hearts rather than utterly ashamed of them?

Does our heavenly Bridegroom expect nothing more of us? Does His mighty all-constraining love intend to do no more for us than to leave us in this deplorable state, when He is undoubtedly able to heal the desperately wicked heart (compare vv. 9 and 14 of Jeremiah 17), to rule the wayward one with His peace, and to establish the fickle one with His grace? Are we not without excuse?

Fixed, trusting in the Lord! Here is the means of the fixing—trust. He works the trust in us by sending the Holy Spirit to reveal God in Christ to us as absolutely, infinitely worthy of our trust. When we see Jesus by Spirit-wrought faith, we cannot but trust Him. We distrust our hearts more truly than ever before, but we trust our Lord entirely, because we trust Him *only*. For entrusting our trust to Him, we know that He is able to keep that which we commit (i.e. entrust) to Him. It is His own way of winning and fixing our hearts for Himself. Is it not a beautiful one? Thus our hearts are established.

But we have not quite faith enough to believe that. So what is the very first doubting, and therefore sad thought that crops up?

"Yes, but I am *afraid* it will not remain fixed."

That is *your* thought. Now see what is God's thought about the case:

"His heart is established, he shall not be afraid" (Ps. 112:8).

Is not that enough? What *is*, if such plain and yet divine words are not? Well, the Gracious One bears with us, and gives line upon line to His poor little children. And so He says, "The peace of God which passeth all understanding shall keep your hearts and minds through Christ Jesus" (Phil. 4:7). And again, "Thy thoughts shall be established" (Prov. 16:3). And again, "Thou wilt keep him in perfect peace, whose mind is stayed on Thee, because he trusteth in Thee" (Isa. 26:3).

And to prove to us that these promises can be realized in present experience, He sends down to us through nearly 3,000 years the words of the man who prayed, "Create in me a clean heart, O God" (Ps. 51:10), and let us hear twice over the new song put by the same Holy Spirit into his mouth; "My heart is fixed, O God, my heart is fixed" (57:7; 108:1).

A Heart Made a Throne

The heart that is established *in* Christ is also established *for* Christ. It becomes His royal throne, no longer occupied by His foe, no longer tottering and unstable. And then we see the beauty and preciousness of the promise, "He shall be a Priest upon His throne" (Zech. 6:13). Not only reigning, but atoning. Not only ruling, but cleansing. Thus the throne is established "in mercy" (Isa. 16:5), but also "by righteousness" (Prov. 16:12).

I think we lose ground sometimes by parleying with the tempter. We have no business to parley with a usurper. The throne is no longer his when we have surrendered it to our Lord Jesus. And why should we allow him to argue with us for one instant, as if it were still an open question?

Don't listen. Simply tell him that Jesus Christ *is* on the long-disputed throne, and no more about it, but turn at once to your King and claim the glorious protection of His sovereignty over you. It is a splendid reality, and you will find it so. He will not abdicate and leave you kingless and defenseless. For verily, "The Lord *is* our King; He will save us" (Isa. 33:22, italics added).

Our hearts are naturally—		*God can make them—*	
Evil	Heb. 3:12	Clean	Ps. 51:10
Desperately wicked	Jer. 17:9	Good	Luke 8:15
Weak	Ezek. 16:30	Fixed	Ps. 112:7
Deceitful	Jer. 17:9	Faithful	Neh. 9:8
Deceived	Isa. 44:20	Understanding	1 Kings 3:9
Double	Ps. 12:2	Honest	Luke 8:15
Impenitent	Rom. 2:5	Contrite	Ps. 51:17
Rebellious	Jer. 5:23	True	Heb. 10:22
Hard	Ezek. 3:7	Soft	Job 23:16
Stony	Ezek. 17:19	New	Ezek. 18:31
Froward	Prov. 17:20	Sound	Ps. 119:80
Despiteful	Ezek. 25:15	Glad	Ps. 16:9
Stout	Isa. 10:12	Established	Ps. 112:8
Haughty	Prov. 18:12	Tender	Eph. 4:32
Proud	Prov. 21:4	Pure	Matt. 5:8
Perverse	Prov. 12:8	Perfect	1 Chron. 29:9
Foolish	Rom. 1:21	Wise	Prov. 11:29

CHAPTER ELEVEN

OUR LOVE
KEPT FOR JESUS

"Keep my love; my Lord, I pour
At Thy feet its treasure-store."

Not as a mere echo from the morning-gilded shore of Tiberias, but as an ever-new, ever-sounding note of divinest power, come the familiar words to each of us, "Lovest thou Me?" (See John 21.) He says it who has loved us with an everlasting love. He says it who has died for us. He says it who has washed us from our sins in His own blood. He says it who has waited for our love, waited patiently all through our coldness.

And if by His grace we have said, "Take my love," which of us has not felt that part of His very answer has been to make us see how little there was to take, and how little of that little has been kept for Him? And yet we *do* love Him! He knows that! The very mourning and longing to love Him more proves it. But we want more than that, and so does our Lord.

Created to Love

He has created us to love. We have a sealed treasure of love, which either remains sealed, and then gradually dries up and wastes away, or is unsealed and poured out, and yet is the fuller and not the emptier for the outpouring. The more love we give, the more we have to give. So far it is only natural. But when the Holy Spirit reveals the love of Christ, and sheds abroad the love of God in our hearts, this natural love is penetrated with a new principle, as it discovers a new Object. Everything that it beholds in that Object gives it new depth and new colors. As it sees the holiness, the beauty, and the glory, it takes the deep hues of conscious sinfulness, unworthiness, and nothingness. As it sees even a glimpse of the love that surpasses knowledge, it takes the glow of wonder and gratitude. And when it sees that love drawing close to its deepest need with blood-purchased pardon, it is intensified and stirred, and there is no more time for weighing and measuring; we must pour it out, all there is of it, with our tears, at the feet that were pierced for love of us.

And what then? Has the flow grown gradually slower and shallower? Has our Lord reason to say, "My brethren have dealt deceitfully as a brook, and as a stream of brooks they pass away"? (Job 6:15) It is humiliating to have found that we could not keep on loving Him, as we loved in that remembered hour when "Thy time was the time of love" (Ezek. 16:8). We have proved that we were not able. Let this be only the stepping-stone to proving that He is able!

There will have been a cause, as we shall see if we seek it honestly. It was that we did not really pour out all our treasure, and so it naturally came to an end. We let it be secretly diverted into other channels. We began keeping back a little part of the price for something else. We looked away from instead of looking unto Jesus. We did not entrust Him with our love and ask Him to keep it for Himself.

And what has He to say to us? Listen! "Thus saith the Lord, 'I remember thee, the kindness of thy youth, the love of thine espousals' " (Jer. 2:2). Can any words be more tender, more touching, to you, to me? Forgetting all the sin, all the backsliding, all the coldness, casting all that into the unreturning depths of the sea. He says He remembers that hour when we first said, "Take my love." He remembers it now, at this minute. He has written it forever on His infinite memory, where the past is as the present.

His own love is unchangeable, so it could never be His wish or will that we should thus drift away from Him. Oh, come and let us return unto the Lord! But is there any hope that, thus returning, our flickering love may be kept from again failing? Hear what He says: "And I will betroth thee unto Me forever" (Hosea 2:19). And again: "Thou *shalt* abide *for Me* many days . . . so will I also be for thee" (3:3, italics added). Shall we trust His Word or not? Is it worthy of our acceptance or not? Oh, rest on this Word of the King, and let Him from this day have the keeping of your love and He will keep it!

Love That Overflows

The love of Christ is not an absorbing, but a radiating love. The more we love Him, the more we shall most certainly love others. Some have not much natural power of loving, but the love of Christ will strengthen it. Some have had the springs of love dried up by some terrible earthquake. They will find fresh springs in Jesus, and the gentle flow will be purer and deeper than the old torrent could ever be. Some have been satisfied that love should rush in a narrow channel, but He will cause it to overflow into many another, and widen its course of blessing. Some have spent all their love on their God-given dear ones. Now He is come whose right it is; and yet in the fullest resumption of that right, He is so gracious that He puts back an even larger measure of the old love into our hand, sanctified with His own love, and energized with His blessing, and strengthened with His new commandment: "That ye love one another, as I have loved you" (John 15:12).

There is no love so deep and wide as that which is kept for Jesus. It flows both fuller and further when it flows only through Him. Then too, it will be a power for Him. It will always be unconsciously working for Him. In drawing others to ourselves by it, we shall be necessarily drawing them nearer to the fountain of our love, never drawing them away from it. It is the great magnet of His love which alone can draw any heart to Him; but when our own are thoroughly yielded to its mighty influence, they will be so magnetized that He will condescend to use them in this way.

Is it not wonderful to think that the Lord Jesus will not only accept and keep, but actually *use* our love?

Of His own have we given Him; for "we love Him because He first loved us" (1 John 4:19).

Set apart to love Him,
And His love to know;
Not to waste affection
On a passing show;
Called to give Him life and heart,
Called to pour the hidden treasure,
Than none other claims to measure,
Into His beloved hand! Thrice blessed "set apart!"

CHAPTER TWELVE

OUR SELVES
KEPT FOR JESUS

*"Keep myself, that I may be
Ever, only, all for Thee."*

"**F**or Thee!" That is the beginning and the end of the whole matter of consecration.

There was a prelude to its endless song—a prelude whose theme is woven into every following harmony in the new anthem of consecrated life: "The Son of God who loved me, and gave Himself *for me*" (Gal. 2:20, italics added). Out of the realized "for me" grows the practical "for Thee"! If the former is a living root, the latter will be its living fruit.

"For *Thee!*" This makes the difference between forced or formal, and therefore, unreasonable service, and reasonable service, which is the beginning of the perfect service where we see His face. This makes the difference between slave work and free work. For Thee, my Redeemer; for Thee, who has spoken to my heart; for Thee, who

98

has done for me—*what?* Let us each pause, and fill in that blank with the great things the Lord has done for us. For Thee, who is to me—*what?* Fill that in too! For Thee, my Saviour Jesus, my Lord and my God!

Surrender of Self

And what is to be for Him? My self. We talk sometimes as if, whatever else could be subdued unto Him, self could never be. Did the Apostle Paul forget to mention this important exception to the "all things" in Philippians 3:21? David said: "Bless the Lord, O my soul, *and all that is within me,* bless His holy name" (Ps. 103:1, italics added). Did he too unaccountably forget to mention that he only meant all that was within him, *except* self? If not, then self must be among the "all things" which the Lord Jesus Christ is able to subdue unto Himself, and which are to bless His holy name. It is self which, once His most treacherous foe, is now, by full and glad surrender, His own soldier—coming over from the rebel camp into the royal army. It is not someone else, some temporarily possessing spirit, which says within us, "Lord, You know that I love Thee," but our true and very self, only changed and renewed by the power of the Holy Spirit. And when we do what we would not, we know that "it is no more *I* that do it, but sin that dwelleth in me" (Rom. 7:20, italics added). Our true self is the new self, taken and won by the love of God, and kept by the power of God.

Yes, *"kept"*! There is the promise on which we ground our prayer; or, rather, one of the promises. For, search and look for your own strengthening and comfort, and you will find it repeated in every part of the Bible, from "I am with thee, and will keep thee," in Genesis 28:15 to "I also will keep thee from the hour of temptation," in Revelation 3:10.

And kept *for Him!* Why should you think it incredible when it is only the fulfilling of His own eternal purpose in creating us? "This people have I formed *for Myself*" (Isa. 43:21, italics added). Not ultimately only, but presently and continually; for He says, "Thou shalt abide *for Me*" (Hosea 3:3, italics added); and, "He that remains, even he, shall be *for our God*" (Zech. 9:7, italics added). Are you one of His people by faith in Jesus Christ? Then see what you are to Him. You, personally and individually, are part of the Lord's portion (Deut. 32:9) and of His inheritance (1 Kings 8:53; Eph. 1:18). His portion and inheritance would not be complete without you. You are His peculiar treasure (Ex. 19:5); a *special* people (how warm, and loving, and natural that expression is!) *"unto Himself"* (Deut. 7:6, italics added). Would you call it "keeping," if you had a special treasure, a darling little child, for instance, and let him run wild into all sorts of dangers all day long, sometimes at your side, and sometimes out in the street, with only the intention of fetching him safely home at night? If ye then, being evil, would know better and do better than that, how much more shall our Lord's keeping be true, and tender, and continual, and effectual, when He declares us to be His peculiar treasure, purchased for Himself at such unknown cost! (See 1 Peter 2:9.)

> He will keep what thus He sought,
> Safely guard the dearly bought;

100

Cherish that which He did choose,
Always love and never lose.

Why Battles Are Lost

I know what some of you are thinking. "Yes; I see it all plainly enough in theory, but in practice I find I am not kept. Self goes over to the other camp again and again. It is not all for Jesus, though I have asked and wished for it to be so."

Dear friends, the *all* must be sealed with *only*. Are you willing to be *only* for Jesus? You have not given all to Jesus while you are not quite ready to be *only* for Him. And it is no use to talk about *ever* while you have not settled the *only* and the *all*. You cannot be for Him, in the full and blessed sense, while you are partly for anything or anybody else. For "the Lord has set apart him that is godly for Himself" (Ps. 4:3). You see, the "for Himself" hinges on the "set apart." There is no consecration without separation. If you are mourning over want of realized consecration, will you look humbly and sincerely into *this* point? "A garden *enclosed* is My sister, My spouse," says the heavenly Bridegroom (Song 4:12, italics added).

But yielding, by His grace, to this blessed setting apart for Himself, "the Lord shall *establish* thee a holy people unto Himself, as He hath sworn unto thee" (Deut. 28:9, italics added). Can there be a stronger promise? Just obey and trust His Word *now*, and yield yourselves *now* unto God, that He may establish you *today* for a people unto Himself. Commit the keeping of your souls to Him in well-doing, as unto a faithful Creator, being persuaded that He is ABLE TO KEEP that which you commit to Him.

101

Now, Lord, I give myself to Thee,
I would be wholly Thine,
As Thou hast given Thyself to me,
And Thou art wholly Mine;
O take me, seal me for Thine own,
Thine altogether, Thine alone.

The Price of Victory

Here comes in once more that immeasurably important subject of our influence. For it is not what we say or do, so much as what we *are*, that influences others. We have heard this, and very likely repeated it again and again, but have we seen it to be inevitably linked with the great question of this chapter? I do not know anything which, thoughtfully considered, makes us realize more vividly the need and the importance of our whole selves being kept for Jesus. Any part not wholly committed, and not wholly kept, must hinder and neutralize the real influence for Him of all the rest. If we ourselves are kept all for Jesus, then our influence will be all kept for Him too. If not, then, however much we may wish and talk and try, we cannot throw our full weight into the right scale. And just insofar as it is not in the one scale, it must be in the other; weighing against the little we have tried to put in the right one, and making the short weight still shorter.

So large a proportion of it is entirely involuntary, while yet the responsibility of it is so enormous, that our helplessness comes out in exceptionally strong relief, while our past debt in this matter is simply incalculable. Are we feeling this a little? Getting just a glimpse, down the misty defiles of memory, of the neutral influence, the wasted influence, the mistaken influence, the actually wrong influence which has marked the ineffaceable although untraceable course? And all the while we owed Him all that influence! It *ought* to have been all for Him!

We have nothing to say. But what has our Lord to say? "I forgave thee all that debt!" (Matt. 18:32)

Then, after that forgiveness which must come first, there comes a thought of great comfort in our freshly felt helplessness, rising out of the very thing that makes us realize this helplessness. Just *because* our influence is to such a great extent involuntary and unconscious, we may rest assured that if we ourselves are truly kept for Jesus, this will be, as a quite natural result, kept for Him also. It cannot be otherwise, for as is the fountain, so will be the flow; as the spring, so the action; as the impulse, so the communicated motion. Thus there may be, and in simple trust there will be, a quiet rest about it, a relief from all sense of strain and effort, a fulfilling of the words, "For he that is entered into His rest, he also hath ceased from his own works as God did from His" (Heb. 4:10). It will not be a matter of *trying* to have good influence, but just of *having* it, as naturally and constantly as the magnetized bar.

Another encouraging thought should follow. Of ourselves we may have but little weight, no particular talents or position or anything else to put into the scale; but let us remember that again and again God has shown that the influence of a very average life, when once really consecrated to Him, may outweigh that of almost any number of merely professing Christians. Such lives are like Gideon's 300 men, carrying not even the ordinary weapons of war, but only trumpets and lamps and empty pitchers, by whom the Lord wrought great deliverance, while He did not use the others at all. "God hath chosen the weak things of the world to confound the things which are mighty" (1 Cor. 1:27).

Should not all this be additional motive for desiring that our *whole* selves should be taken and kept?

* * * * *

"I know that whatsoever God doeth, it shall be forever" (Ecc. 3:14). Therefore we may rejoicingly say "ever" as well as "only" and "all for Thee"! For the Lord is our Keeper, and He is the Almighty and the Everlasting God, "with whom is no variableness, neither shadow of turning" (James 1:17). He will never change His mind about keeping us, and no man is able to pluck us out of His hand (see John 10:28-29). Neither will Christ let us pluck ourselves out of His hand. Indeed, "He that keepeth us will not slumber" (Ps. 121:3). Once having undertaken His vineyard, He will keep it night and day, till all the days and nights are over, and we know the full meaning of the salvation ready to be revealed in the last time, unto which we are kept by His power.

And then, forever for Him! Passing from the gracious keeping by faith for this little while, to the glorious keeping in His presence for all eternity! Forever fulfilling the object for which He formed us and chose us, we showing forth His praise, and He showing the exceeding riches of His grace toward us in the ages to come! *He for us and we for Him forever!* Oh, how little we can grasp this! Yet this is the fruition of being "kept for Jesus"!

CHAPTER THIRTEEN

CHRIST FOR US

The typical promise, "Thou shalt abide for Me many days" (Hosea 3:3), is indeed a marvel of love. For it is given to the most undeserving, described under the strongest possible figure of utter worthlessness and treacherousness—the woman beloved, yet an adulteress.

The depth of the abyss shows the length of the line that has fathomed it, yet only the length of the line reveals the real depth of the abyss. The sin shows the love and the love reveals the sin. The Bible has few words more touching, though seldom quoted, than those just preceding this wonderful promise: "The love of the Lord toward the Children of Israel, who look to other gods and love flagons of wine" (3:1). Put that into the personal application which no doubt underlies it and this Scripture teaches, "The love of the Lord toward *me*, who hath looked away from Him, with wandering, faithless eyes, to other helps and hopes, and has loved earthly joys and sought earthly gratifications—the love of the Lord toward even me!" And then hear Him saying in the next verse, "So I bought her to me" (3:2); stooping to do *that* in His unspeakable condescension of love, not with the typical silver and barley, but with the precious blood of Christ. Then, having thus loved us, and rescued us, and bought us with a price indeed, He says, still under the same figure, "Thou shalt abide for Me many days."

This is both a command and a pledge. But the very pledge implies our past unfaithfulness, and the proved need of even our own part being undertaken by the ever patient Lord. He Himself has to guarantee our faithfulness, because there is no other hope of our continuing faithful. Well may such love win our full and glad surrender, and such a promise win our happy and confident trust!

Our Every Need

But our Saviour says more. He says, "So will I also be for thee!" (3:3) And this seems an even greater marvel of love, as we observe how He meets every detail of our consecration with these wonderful words.

1. *His Life* for thee! "The Good Shepherd giveth His life for the sheep" (John 10:11). Oh, wonderful gift! Not promised, but *given;* not to friends, but to enemies. Given without condition, without reserve, without return! Himself unknown and unloved, His gift unsought and unasked, He gave His life for thee; a more than royal bounty—the greatest gift that Deity could devise. Oh,

grandeur of love! "I lay down My life for the sheep!"
(10:15) And we for whom He gave it have held back, and
hesitated to give our lives, not even *for* Him (He has not
asked us to do that), but *to* Him! But that is past, and He
has tenderly pardoned the unloving, ungrateful reserve,
and has graciously accepted the poor little fleeting breath
and speck of dust which was all we had to offer. And now
His precious death and His glorious life are all for thee.

2. *His Eternity* for thee. All we can ask Him to take are
days and moments—the little span given us as it is given,
and of this only the present in deed and the future in will.
As for the past, insofar as we did not give it to Him, it is
too late; we can never give it now! But His past was given
to us, though ours was not given to Him. Oh, what a
tremendous debt this shows us!

Way back in the dim depths of past eternity, before the
earth and the worlds were made, His divine existence in
the bosom of His Father was all for thee, purposing and
planning for thee, receiving and holding the promise of
eternal life for thee.

Then the thirty-three years among sinners on this sinful
earth: do we think enough of the slowly wearing days and
nights, the heavy-footed hours, the never-hastening min-
utes, that went to make up those thirty-three years of trial
and humiliation? We all know how slowly time passes
when suffering and sorrow are near, and there is no
reason to suppose that our Master was exempted from
this part of our infirmities.

Then His present is for thee. Even now He lives to
make intercession; even now He thinks about you; even
now He knows, He cares, He loves.

Then, only to think that His whole eternity will be for thee! Millions of ages of unfoldings of all His love, and of ever new declarings of His Father's name to His brethren. Think of it! And can we ever hesitate to give *all* of our poor little hours to His service?

3. *His Hands* for thee. Literal hands; literally pierced, when the whole weight of His quivering frame hung from their torn muscles and bared nerves; literally uplifted in parting blessing. Consecrated, priestly hands; filled hands (Ex. 28:41; 29:9; etc., margin)—filled once with His great offering, and now with gifts and blessings for thee. Tender hands, touching and healing, lifting and leading with gentlest care. Strong hands, upholding and defending. Open hands, filling with good and satisfying desire (Pss. 104:28; 145:16). Faithful hands, restraining and sustaining. "His left hand is under my head, and His right hand doth embrace me" (Song 2:6).

4. *His Feet* for thee. They were weary very often; they were wounded and bleeding once. They made clear footprints as He went about doing good, and as He went up to Jerusalem to suffer; and these blessed steps of His most holy life, both as substitution and example, were for thee. Our place of waiting and learning, of resting and loving, is at His feet. And still those blessed feet are and shall be for thee, until He comes again to receive us unto Himself, until and when the Word is fulfilled, "They shall walk with me in white" (Rev. 3:4).

5. *His Voice* for thee. The "voice of my beloved that knocks, saying, 'Open, to Me, My sister, My love'" (Song 5:2); the voice that His sheep hear and know, and that calls out the fervent response, "Master, say on!" (Luke

7:40) This is not all. It was the literal voice of the Lord
Jesus which uttered that one echoless cry of desolation on
the cross for thee, and it will be His own literal voice
which will say, "Come, ye blessed!" (Matt. 25:34) to thee.
And that same tender and glorious voice has literally sung
and will sing for thee. I think He consecrated song for us,
and made it a sweet and sacred thing forever, when He
Himself sang a hymn, the very last thing before He went
forth to consecrate suffering for us.

That was not His last song. "The Lord thy God . . . will
joy over thee with singing" (Zeph. 3:17). And the time is
coming when He will not only sing for thee or over thee,
but with thee. He says He will: "In the midst of the
church will I sing praise unto Thee!" (Heb. 2:12) Now
what a magnificent glimpse of joy this is! Jesus Himself
leading the praises of His brethren, and we ourselves
singing not merely in such a chorus, but with such a
leader! If singing *for* Jesus is such delight here, what will
this singing *with* Jesus be? Surely song may well be a holy
thing to us henceforth.

6. *His Lips* for thee. Perhaps there is no part of our
consecration which it is so difficult practically to realize,
and in which it is, therefore, so needful to recollect—"I
also for thee." It is often helpful to read straight through
one or more of the Gospels with a special thought on our
mind, and see how much bears upon it. When we read
one through with this thought—"His *lips* for me!"—wondering, verse by verse, at the grace which was poured
into them, and the gracious words which fell from them,
wondering more and more at the cumulative force and
infinite wealth of tenderness and power and wisdom and

109

love flowing from them, we cannot but desire that our lips and all the fruit of them should be wholly for Him. For thee they were opened in blessing; for thee they were closed when He was led as a lamb to the slaughter. And whether teaching, warning, giving counsel, comfort, or encouragement, commandments in whose keeping there is a great reward, or promises which exceed all we ask or think—all the precious fruit of His lips is for thee, really and truly meant for thee.

7. *His Wealth* for thee. "Though He was rich, yet for your sakes He became poor, that ye through His poverty might be rich" (2 Cor. 8:9). Yes, through His poverty the unsearchable riches of Christ are for thee. Sevenfold riches are mentioned; and these are no unminted treasure or sealed reserve, but ready coin for our use, stamped with His own image and superscription, and poured freely into the hand of faith. The mere list is wonderful. Riches of goodness, riches of forbearance and long-suffering, riches both of wisdom and knowledge, riches of mercy, exceeding riches of grace, and riches of glory! And His own Word says, "All are yours!" (1 Cor. 3:22) Glance on in faith, and think of eternity flowing on and on beyond the mightiest sweep of imagination, and realize that all His riches in glory and the riches of His glory are and shall be for thee!

In view of this, shall we care to reserve anything that rust corrupts for ourselves?

8. *His Treasures of Wisdom and Knowledge* for thee. First, used for our behalf and benefit. Why did He expend such immeasurable might of mind on a world which is to be burned up, but that He would fit it perfectly to be, not the

home, but the school of His children? The infinity of His skill is such that the most powerful intellects find a lifetime too short to penetrate a little way into a few secrets of some one small department of His working. If we turn to Providence, it is quite enough to take only one's own life, and look at it microscopically and telescopically, and marvel at the treasures of wisdom lavished upon its details, ordering and shaping and fitting the tiny confused bits into the true mosaic which He means it to be. Many a little thing in our lives reveals the same. Mind, which adjusted a perfect proportion in the delicate hinges of the snowdrop and the droop of its bell, with the mass of the globe and the force of gravitation. How kind we think it if a very talented friend spends a little of his thought and power of mind in teaching us or planning for us! Have we been grateful for the infinite thought and wisdom which our Lord has expended on us and our creation, preservation, and redemption?

Secondly, to be shared with us. He says, "All that I have is thine" (Luke 15:31). He holds nothing back, reserves nothing from His dear children, and what we cannot receive now He is keeping for us. He gives us hidden riches of secret places now, but by and by He will give us more, and the glorified intellect will be filled continually out of His treasures of wisdom and knowledge. But the sanctified intellect will be, must be, used for Him, and only for Him, now!

9. *His Will* for thee. Think first of the *infinite might* of that will; the first great law and the first great force of the universe, from which alone every other law and every other force has sprung, and to which all are subordinate.

111

"[He] worketh all things after the counsel of His own will" (Eph. 1:11). "He doeth according to His will in the army of heaven, and among the inhabitants of the earth" (Dan. 4:35).

Then think of the *infinite mysteries* of that will. For ages and generations the hosts of heaven have wonderingly watched its vouchsafed unveilings and its sublime developments, and still they are waiting, watching, and wondering.

Creation and providence are but the whisper of its power, but redemption is its music, and praise is the echo which shall yet fill His temple. The whisper and the music, yes, and the thunder of His power, are all for thee. For what *is* the good pleasure of His will? (Eph. 1:5) Oh, what a grand list of blessings, purposed, provided, purchased, and possessed, all flowing to us out of it! And nothing but blessings, nothing but privileges, which we never should have imagined, and which, even when revealed, we are slow of heart to believe; nothing but what should even now fill us with joy unspeakable and full of glory!

Think of this will as always and altogether on our side—always working for us, and in us, and with us, if we will only let it; think of it as always and only synonymous with infinitely wise and almighty love; think of it as undertaking all for us, from the great work of our eternal salvation down to the momentary details of guidance and supply: and do we not feel utter shame and self-abhorrence at *ever* having hesitated for an instant to give up our tiny, feeble, blind will to be—not crushed, not even bent, but *blent* with His glorious and perfect will?

10. *His Heart* for thee. "Behold . . . He is mighty . . . in heart," said Job (Job 36:5, margin). And this mighty and tender heart is for thee! If He had only stretched forth His hand to save us from bare destruction, and said, "My hand for thee!" how could we have praised Him enough? But what shall we say of the unspeakably marvelous condescension which says, "Thou hast ravished (margin, *taken away*) My heart, My sister, My spouse!" (Song 4:9) The very fountain of His divine life, and light, and love, the very center of His being, is given to His beloved ones, who are not only set as a seal upon His heart, but taken into His heart, so that our lives are hid there, and we dwell there in the very center of all safety, and power, and love, and glory.

What will be the revelation of that day, when the Lord Jesus promises, "Ye shall know that I am in My Father, and *ye in Me*"? (John 14:20, italics added) For He implies that we do not yet know it, and that our present knowledge of this dwelling in Him is not knowledge at all compared with what He is going to show us about it.

Now shall we, can we, reserve any corner of our hearts from Him?

11. *His Love* for thee. Not a passive, possible love, but outflowing, yes *outpouring* of the real, glowing, personal love of His mighty and tender heart. Love, not as an attribute, a quality, a latent force, but an acting, moving, reaching, touching, and grasping power. Love, not a cold, beautiful, far-off star, but a sunshine that comes and enfolds us, making us warm and glad, and strong and bright and fruitful.

His love! What manner of love is it? What should be

quoted to prove or describe it? First the whole Bible with its mysteries and marvels of redemption, then the whole book of providence and the whole volume of creation. Then add to these the unknown records of eternity past and the unknown glories of eternity to come. Then let the immeasurable quotation be sung by angels and archangels, and all the company of heaven, with all the harps of God, and still that love will be untold, still it will be the love of Christ that surpasses knowledge. But it is for thee!

12. *Himself* for thee. Christ also hath loved us, and given Himself for us. "The Son of God . . . loved me, and gave Himself for me" (Gal. 2:20). Yes, Himself! What is the bride's true and central treasure? What calls forth the deepest, brightest, sweetest thrill of love and praise? Not the Bridegroom's priceless gifts, not the robe of His resplendent righteousness, not the dowry of unsearchable riches, not the magnificence of the palace home to which He is bringing her, not the glory which she shall share with Him, but HIMSELF! Jesus Christ, "who His own self bare our sins in His own body on the tree" (1 Peter 2:24); this same Jesus, whom having not seen, we love (see 1:8); the Son of God, and the Man of sorrows; my Saviour, my Friend, my Master, my King, my Priest, my Lord and my God—He says, "*I* also for thee!" What an "*I*"! What power and sweetness we feel in it, so different from any human "I," for all His Godhead and all His manhood are concentrated in it; and all for thee!

And not only *all*, but *ever* for thee! His unchangeableness is the seal upon every attribute; He will be this same Jesus forever. How can mortal mind estimate this enormous promise? How can mortal heart conceive what is enfolded in these words, "I also for thee"?

One glimpse of its fullness and glory, and we feel that henceforth it must be, shall be, and by His grace *will* be our truehearted, wholehearted cry—

Take *my self*, and I will be
Ever, ONLY, ALL for Thee!